Curious George™
Adventures in Learning

Dear Mom or Dad,

This **story-based workbook series** was designed by Houghton Mifflin Harcourt, a global leader in education serving 60 million students worldwide.

Just like George, your child is naturally curious. When stacking blocks or stomping puddles, he or she is learning about the world. This book introduces concepts in a way that is natural to your child—through **real-world exploration**.

12 learning adventures provide the backdrop for math, reading, and science practice. When activities are framed around *real life*, children are more motivated to ask, learn, and retain new information.

This book also folds in social and emotional activities to help children adapt to new environments, work with peers, and express their feelings.

Don't forget—*you* are part of the adventure! Look for the **blue bird** throughout the book. That's your cue to:

- Read a story together.

- Relate the story to a shared experience.

- Celebrate your child's achievements.

- Play a learning game together.

Edited by Sharon Emerson

Reviewed by Alessandra Preziosi; HMH Studios Math & Science Learning Architecture team

Copyright © 2014 HMH Consumer Company. All rights reserved.

CURIOUS GEORGE and related characters, created by Margret and H. A. Rey, are copyrighted and trademarked by Houghton Mifflin Harcourt Publishing Company. Illustrations copyright © 2014 by Houghton Mifflin Harcourt Publishing Company. All rights reserved.

A limited permission to reproduce portions of this work is granted to classroom teachers for classroom use only, not for commercial resale, by virtue of the purchase of the book. Except as otherwise set forth herein, no part of this work may be reproduced or transmitted in any form or by any electronic or mechanical means (including photocopying, recording, or information storage or retrieval) without prior written permission of the publisher.

Send all inquiries to: Permissions, Houghton Mifflin Harcourt Publishing Company, 215 Park Avenue South, New York, New York 10003

ISBN: 9780544373235

www.hmhco.com

Manufactured in the United States of America

DOM 10 9 8 7 6 5 4 3 2 1

4500511301

Curious George™
Adventures in Learning

Houghton Mifflin Harcourt
Boston   New York

Adventures in Learning

Baseball

George is curious about . . .

 Reading   sequence words;
compound words

 Math   flat and solid shapes;
measuring height

 Science   motion and speed;
animal parts

 Social and   sportsmanship
Emotional

Take Me Out to the Ball Game

George was excited.
The man with the yellow hat
was taking him to a baseball game!

George cheered for
the Mudville Miners.

Pop! When a Miner hit the ball,
George jumped up and down.

Whoosh! When a Miner swung
and missed the ball, George groaned.

A woman walked through the stands
with a camera. She pointed it at the fans.
They showed up on a big TV screen
across the field.

George wanted to be on TV, too.
So he jumped in front of the camera.
But he was too short to show up
on the big screen.

Do you belong to a team? What is the name of the team?
Can you name another team sport?

George had an idea.
He got very close to the camera.
He looked into the lens
and smiled.

A Miner hit the ball, but nobody noticed.
The fans were now watching George.

After the game, the Miners invited George into the dugout. They wanted to meet the monkey who was on the big screen.

They may have won the baseball game. But George was the star of the day.

What did George do to show up on the big screen?
A team sits in a dugout. Why do you think there are two dugouts in a baseball stadium?

1, 2, 3 . . . Silly As Can Be

The baseball coach is not making a funny face. He is using hand signs to tell the players what to do. George makes signs, too!

First, he wiggles his ears.
Next, he pats his tummy.
Last, he touches his chin.

Write **1**, **2**, and **3** to show the correct order.

_____   _____   _____

Draw pictures of George in the correct order.

First, George covers his eyes. **Next**, he touches his nose. **Last**, he sticks out his tongue.

Throw the Ball

Trace the words.

First   Next   Last

Write **First**, **Next**, and **Last** to tell George
how to throw a ball.

_____
_____, raise your arm back.

_____
_____, quickly move your arm forward.

_____
_____, let go of the ball.

Draw yourself throwing a ball to George.

In the Dugout

A **compound word** is made up of two smaller words. Make a compound word to describe each picture.

ball　　**foot**　　**pop**　　**score**

_____
base _____

_____
_____ corn

_____
_____ board

_____
_____ ball

16

Write the words that make up each
compound word.

homerun = _____ + _____

ladybug = _____ + _____

playground = _____ + _____

raincoat = _____ + _____

shoelace = _____ + _____

Look at the picture of each compound word.
Draw the missing picture.

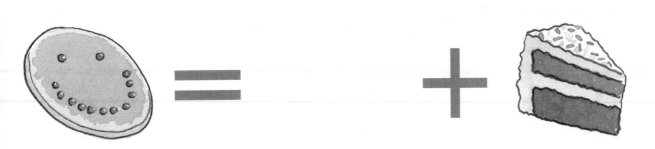

Play Ball!

Tell what is happening at the game.
Choose a word to complete each sentence.

ball   **batter**   **cheer**   **pitcher**   **team**

The _____ throws the ball.

The _____ swings the bat.

The _____ flies far.

The fans _____ .

Their _____ is winning!

The camera is
pointed at you!
Draw yourself
cheering.

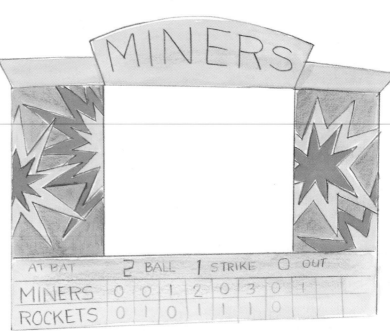

MINERS								
AT BAT		2 BALL		1 STRIKE		0 OUT		
MINERS	0	0	1	2	0	3	0	1
ROCKETS	0	1	0	1	1	1	0	

18

Fly Ball!

Write the missing word in each sentence.

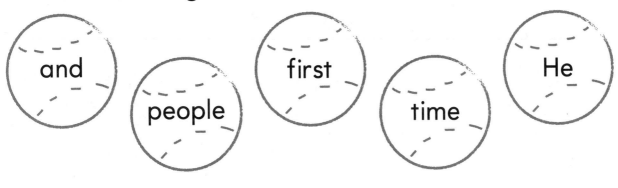

and

people

first

time

He

The batter swings _____ misses.

_____ swings again.

This _____, he hits the ball.

He runs to _____ base.

The _____ cheer.

Connect the Shapes

Draw a line from each flat shape to a solid shape.
Then draw a line from the solid shape to an object.

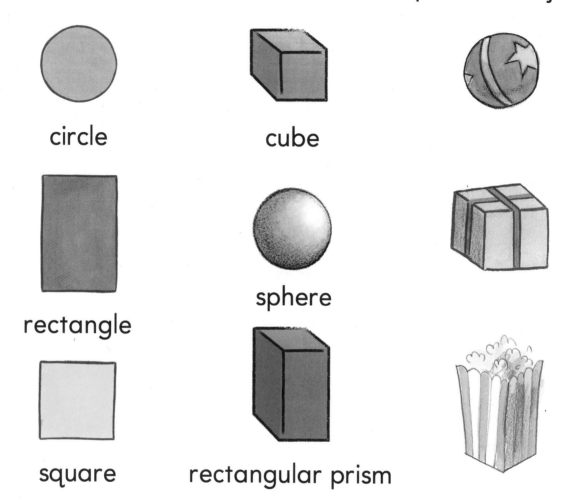

circle

cube

rectangle

sphere

square

rectangular prism

One ball is not a sphere. Make an **X** on it.

How Tall?

George is about 5 baseballs tall.
About how tall is each friend?

Write a number.

about _____ ⚾   about _____ ⚾   about _____ ⚾

One friend is about 5 baseballs taller than George.
Circle him above.

How tall are you? _____

I am about _____ ⚾ tall.

Fast and Slow

Speed is the measure of how fast something moves.
Circle things that move **fast**.
Make an **X** on things that move **slowly**.

Tell how George is moving.
Use a word below or one of your own.

running   **sliding**

_____   _____
_____   _____

Playtime

George plays outside. Look at what he is wearing. Draw a line to the **animal part** that does the same thing.

A **helmet** protects George's head.

a wooly coat

Flippers help George move underwater.

a hard shell

A **snowsuit** keeps George warm.

fins

One animal has **four wide feet** to help it walk on sand. Circle it.

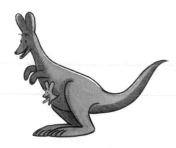

A Good Sport!

Circle the words that tell how George is a good sport.

George (**breaks** / **follows**) the rules of the game.

George is (**nice** / **mean**) to the other team.

George does not get (**mad** / **silly**) when he loses a game.

The Miners win! What should they say to the losing team?

Write it.

_____

_____

Good game!   Nice job!

You did it!

Make an **X** next to things you know.

Place a sticker

- [ ] I can use the words **first**, **next**, and **last** to explain how to throw a ball.

- [ ] I can put small words together to make bigger, or **compound**, words.

- [ ] I learned the new words **batter**, **pitcher**, and **team**.

- [ ] I can compare **flat** and **solid** shapes.

- [ ] I can measure **height** using a baseball.

- [ ] I can use the words **fast** and **slow** to describe **speed**.

- [ ] I know that animals have special **body parts** to keep them safe or **warm**.

- [ ] I know how to be a **good sport**.

Turn the page to start a new adventure!

Animal Shelter

George is curious about . . .

 **Reading**   comparing and contrasting; consonant digraphs; high-frequency words

 **Math**   bar graphs; making tens and ones

 **Science**   animals caring for young; life cycle

 **Social and Emotional**   caring for pets

Here, Kitty, Kitty!

It was a sunny day. George and the man with the yellow hat went for a walk.

Meow. Meow.

George was curious.
What was making that sound?

George and the man looked around.
They did not see anything.

Just then, the bush started to wiggle.
A kitten poked her head out.

Meow.

Where was the kitten?
Why do you think the kitten was hiding?

George and the man searched for the kitten's family. But she was alone.

"This cat is too young to be by herself," said the man. "She needs a home."

George scratched his head.
How would she find one?

"Let's bring her to the animal shelter,"
said the man. "They can keep her safe
until she finds a home."

Where do George and the man take the kitten?
What can the shelter do for the cat?

George carried
the kitten
to the shelter.

"Come inside," said the director.
"We will take good care of this kitten.
We will give her food, water, and a
warm place to sleep."

George visited the animals inside.
He saw bunnies, a dog, and more cats.
They were all waiting to find homes.

George smiled. He knew that the
shelter would keep them safe until
a family came to take them home.

Look at the animals. Which ones might live in the wild?
Why might there be a wild animal in a shelter?

Meow! Woof!

Compare the animals. Read each sentence.
Check the box if it describes the animal.
Then circle if they are **alike** or **different**.

It has a tail. ☐ ☐ **alike** **different**

It has fur. ☐ ☐ **alike** **different**

It meows. ☐ ☐ **alike** **different**

It barks. ☐ ☐ **alike** **different**

Both animals have ears. Tell how they are **different**.
Complete the sentence.

The cat has _____ ears, but

the dog has _____ ears.

At Home or in the Park?

Where does George do these things?
Look at each picture. Write **home** or **park**.

He eats
breakfast here. _____

He plays on
the swings here. _____

He goes to
sleep here. _____

He has a
picnic here. _____

He plays with
his toys here. _____

Compare and Contrast

35

Shadow the Cat

Shadow starts with the **sh** sound.
Say the name of each picture.
Circle pictures that start with the **sh** sound.

Shadow

Did you get three in a row? Draw a line.

A Good Shelter

A shelter takes care of animals.
There are shelters for all kinds of animals.
Write **sh** or **ch** to finish the animal names.

_____ eep

_____ fi _____

_____ ick

ostri _____

37

Who Am I?

Draw a line from the clue to the picture.

He has a tail.
He eats grass.

She lives in a nest.
She can fly.

He can carry a bone.
He likes to bark.

He is curious!

Eat, Play, Love

Trace each word. Then circle the picture that matches each word.

eat

play

love

George's Scrapbook

George made a scrapbook.
Choose a word to write under each picture.

kitten   **search**   **shelter**   **walk**

_____
- - - - - - - - - - - -
_____

_____
- - - - - - - - - - - -
_____

_____
- - - - - - - - - - - -
_____

_____
- - - - - - - - - - - -
_____

40

Cats and Dogs

Are there more cats or dogs? Find out.
Color a square for each cat.
Color a square for each dog.

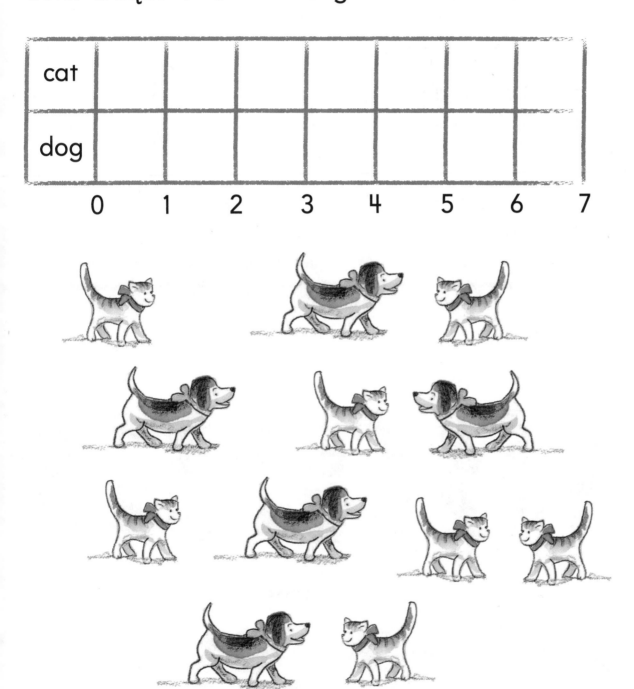

cat							
dog							

0   1   2   3   4   5   6   7

There are _____ more cats than dogs.

Count the Animals

George counts 12 balls at the shelter.

12 = ____ ten ____ ones

Now count the animals.
Write the number in tens and ones.

____ ____

____ ten ____ ones

____

____ ten ____ ones

____ ____

____ tens ____ ones

Animal Treats

Each box has 10 treats.
Write the number of treats in tens and ones.

__3__ tens __2__ ones

__32__ treats

____ ten ____ ones

____ treats

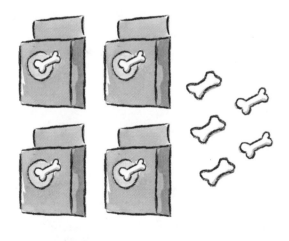 

____ tens ____ ones

____ treats

____ tens ____ ones

____ treats

43

Who Takes Care of Us?

Animal parents take care of their babies.
Draw a line from each sentence to a picture.

She teaches
her baby to find nuts.

She feeds
her baby a worm.

She feeds her baby
plants and twigs.

The man with the yellow hat takes care of George.
Draw who takes care of you.

Animals Caring for Young

44

We All Grow Up

Draw a line from the baby to the adult.

What Does It Need?

Do you want to take care of an animal?
Circle one.

Make an **X** next to things it needs to **grow**
and **stay healthy**.

☐ **air** to breathe

☐ **water** to drink

☐ **food** to eat

☐ a clean **shelter**

☐ **space** to exercise and play

Look at the list again.
Draw a line under things **you** need to grow and
stay healthy.

You did it!

Make an **X** next to things you know.

Place a sticker

☐ I can tell how a cat and a dog are **alike** and **different**.

☐ I know the sounds **sh** and **ch** as in **sheep** and **chick**.

☐ I know the words **eat**, **play**, and **love** on sight.

☐ I can make a **bar graph**.

☐ I know that **12** is **1 ten** and **2 ones**.

☐ I know that some animal parents **feed** their babies and keep them **safe**.

☐ I know that animals **grow** and **change**. I grow and change, too!

☐ I know how to take care of animals. They need **food** and **water**. A happy kitten *purrs*!

Turn the page to start a new adventure!

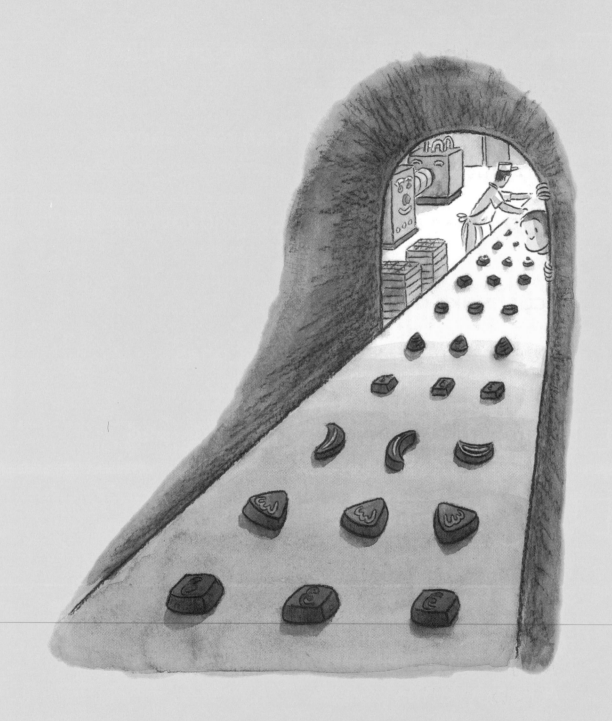

Factory

George is curious about . . .

Reading   story details; sensory words;
                 high-frequency words

Math   adding 3 numbers;
                 adding to with pictures

Science   healthful eating;
                 sense of taste;
                 being active

Social and   listening
Emotional

The Chocolate Factory

One afternoon, George and the man
with the yellow hat took a drive.
Sniff, sniff. George smelled something.
It was chocolate!

The man pointed to a big building.
It was a chocolate factory.

"They must be making chocolates today!"
said the man. "Let's buy a treat."
George loved chocolates!

 A factory can make candy, crayons, and pencils.
What else is made in a factory?

George and the man walked into the
factory store. There were round treats
and square treats. One treat looked
like a bunny.

The factory made them all. *But how?*
George heard *Chug! Chug! Chug!*
He walked toward the noise.

George looked at the factory floor.
There was a shiny machine.
Chocolates came out of the machine on a
moving belt. Workers put them into boxes.

George tried to count the chocolates.
One, two, three, four, five . . .
He lost count. The belt moved too fast!

What do you think happens inside the machine?
Where do you think the chocolate goes after being boxed?

Some chocolates started to fall off the end of the belt. A worker shouted, "Help! We need more hands!"

George wanted to help! He had two hands *and* two feet.

George caught some chocolates with his feet. He put those into boxes. He caught some chocolates in his hands. Those, he ate!

The factory worker wanted to thank George for his help. "Here is a box of chocolate!" he said. George rubbed his tummy. He loved chocolate, but he had eaten enough . . .

. . . at least for today!

Why does George have a tummy ache?
Did you ever eat too much of something? How did you feel?

George Dreams

George dreams about his day at the factory.
Underline the sentences that describe
what he saw.

The chocolates moved on a belt.

The belt moved slowly.

The workers wore white hats.

They also wore blue aprons.

They put the chocolates into boxes.

Brush Up, George!

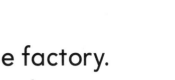

George ate a lot of candy at the factory.
He brushed his teeth when he got home.
Draw a line from each word
to its picture.

bathrobe

comb

mirror

pajamas

sink

toilet

toothbrush

toothpaste

Sniff! Sniff!

George uses his **senses** to learn about the world. Choose a word to complete each sentence.

hears   sees   smells   tastes   touches

George _____ a sweet treat.

George _____ the color brown.

George _____ sticky caramel.

George _____ a loud whistle.

George _____ fresh air.

Circle the body part George uses to smell chocolate.

My Factory

George visited a chocolate factory.
Imagine that you have a factory.
First decide what it makes.

_____

My factory makes _____.

Now draw it.

What color is the thing
your factory makes?

What does it feel like?
Is it soft, bumpy,
or something else?

_____

_____

What does it taste like?

_____

_____

What does it smell like?

Banana Cream

Use these words to complete the story.

just **like** **of** **one** **takes**

George opens a box _____ candy.

He picks _____.

It looks _____ a banana.

George _____ a bite.

It tastes _____ like a banana.

Mmm!

Fun at the Factory

Find these words in the puzzle.

away   good   help   puts   soon   thank

```
s  o  o  n  m  o  f
h  i  a  w  a  y  t
e  e  p  b  b  i  h
l  g  o  o  d  o  a
p  p  b  h  g  p  n
a  p  u  t  s  e  k
r  j  w  i  b  n  g
```

Complete the story with the words you found.

George is a _____ monkey.

He wants to _____ the workers.

He _____ the chocolates into boxes.

The workers _____ George.

George and the man drive _____.

"Come back _____!" call the workers.

This or That?

Read each question. Then write the answer.

Do people **work**
or **play** at a factory?
_____

Is chocolate a **sweet**
or **salty** snack?
_____

Is a machine a **person**
or a **thing**?
_____

Does a worker do a **job**
or take a **nap**?
_____

Does a tummy ache
feel **good** or **bad**?
_____

Candy Counter

Count the candies.
Circle two numbers to add first.
Write the sum. Then write the total sum.

3 + 2 + 1 =

3 +

5 + 6 + 1 =

2 + 10 + 4 =

8 + 4 + 4 =

3 + 4 + 5 =

9 + 1 + 3 =

11 + 4 + 2 =

7 + 6 + 2 =

8 + 3 + 6 =

3 + 3 + 4 =

Heart-shaped Box

Draw the correct number of chocolates
in each box.

10   14

Draw 3 more chocolates in each box.
Then write how many.

Use Pictures to Add To

Yummy Tummy!

George has a tummy ache.
Circle healthy snacks for George.

Sense of Taste

Taste It!

George can taste to learn if something is sweet, sour, or salty.
Draw a line to a snack with the same taste.

 It's **sweet!**

 It's **sour!**

 It's **salty!**

My favorite food is _____.

It tastes
(Circle one.)

66

At Work and Play

George loses water from his body
when he **breathes** and **sweats**.
Help George replace the water he lost.
Draw a silly straw from the drink to George.

Circle how you like to be active.

George Listens

The man is talking to George.
Check the ways George listens.

☐ He stops what he is doing.

☐ He looks at the man.

☐ He listens.

Circle who is listening. Can you find all 17?

You did it!

Make an X next to things you know.

Place a sticker

☐ I can remember story details.

☐ I can **hear**, **see**, **smell**, **taste**, and **touch** to learn about the world.

☐ I know the words **good**, **help**, and **thank** on sight.

☐ I learned the new words **factory**, **machine**, and **worker**.

☐ I can add three numbers.

☐ I can **add to** using pictures.

☐ I can pick out healthy snacks.

☐ I can describe if something tastes **salty**, **sweet**, or **sour**.

☐ I know that I should drink water after I am active.

☐ I listen with my eyes and ears. When I listen, I am quiet.

Turn the page to start a new adventure!

Movies

George is curious about . . .

Reading   fact and fiction;
singular and plural nouns;
noun and verb agreement;
high-frequency words

Math   addition; telling time
in hours and half hours

Science   light and shadow

**Social and   feelings
Emotional**

Lights! Camera! STOMP!

George went to the movies with his friend,
the man with the yellow hat.
There was a dinosaur double feature!

The first movie was about
Triceratops — a large beast!

It ate a lot.
That made George hungry.

Tri– means three. How many movies does a triple feature have?
What does Triceratops have three of?

The man gave George
some money.
When the first movie
ended, George ran
to the snack bar.

He returned with
a large bucket
of popcorn.

It was big enough to feed himself,
the man, and a Triceratops!

The second movie started.
A Tyrannosaurus rex
stomped across
the screen.

ROAR!

George jumped up
in his seat.
It sounded like
there was a dinosaur
in the movie theater!

George bought a large bucket of popcorn.
What are other popcorn sizes?

George peeked behind his seat.
There was no dinosaur — just people.
They were laughing and smiling!

The dinosaur was *big*.
The dinosaur was *loud*.
But it was not real.

On the way out, George rex
stomped and roared.
The man held onto the small
dinosaur's hand.

Why did George think there was a real dinosaur in the theater?
How do you pretend to be a dinosaur?

Double Feature

A movie poster can tell you about the story.
Which story is made-up? Circle the clue.

A story about
real life has **facts**.

A made-up
story is **fiction**.

Read about each story.
Make an **X** next to stories about **real life**.

☐ A family takes a trip together.

☐ A dinosaur goes to school.

☐ A mother lion takes care of her cub.

☐ A dog wins a gold medal at the Olympics.

☐ A monkey grows up in the jungle.

Let's Pretend

Change each sentence from fact to fiction.
Replace the underlined words
with your own words.

Fact. George rode the bus
to the <u>city</u>.

Fiction. George rode the bus
_____
to the _____ moon _____!

Fact. The dogs <u>ran</u> to the park.

Fiction. The dogs
_____
_____
to the park!

Fact. George saw a <u>duck</u>
outside his window.

Fiction. George saw a
_____
_____
outside his window!

Two Tickets, Please!

Add **-s** to each word to show more than one.

ticket   _tickets_

dinosaur _____

monkey   _____

hat   _____

bucket   _____ of popcorn!

Find words that mean more than one.
Color in those tickets.

show

movies

drink

straws

screen

seats

stars

lights

More, Please!

George wants more than one. Rewrite each word to mean more than one. Add **–s** or **–es**.

snack_____   box_____

dish_____   kiss_____

lunch_____   dime_____

_____

George wants two _____.
Draw them.

You can add **–s** to most words
to show more than one.
Add **–es** if the word ends with **s**, **x**, **ch** or **sh**.

George in the Movies

George is going to be a movie star! Write the correct words to find out what happened.

"I _____ you
in my next picture!"

want   wants

George _____ his name on the contract.

write   writes

Now George _____ on the film set.

is   are

The set _____ like a jungle!

look   looks

People _____ to see the movie.

come   comes

George _____, too!

go   goes

Shh! The movie _____ starting.

is   are

The people _____ talking.

stop   stops

George _____ on the big screen.

is   are

The people _____ for George!

clap   claps

Cowboy George

George dreams that he is in a cowboy movie.
Find each word in the pictures.
Then color it in.

all   big   him   see   has   you

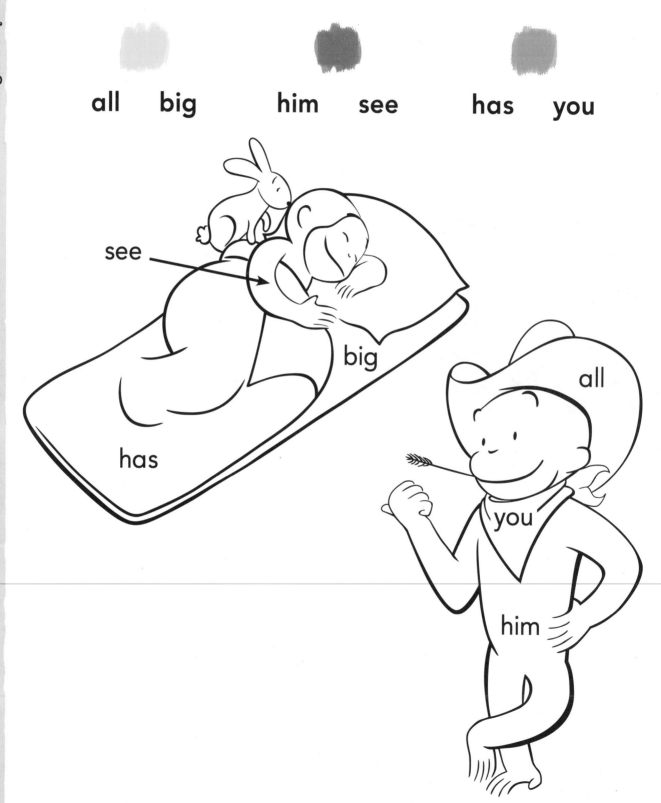

see

big

has

all

you

him

84

Word Crunch

Find these words in the puzzle.

are	**every**	**want**	**your**
y	q	a	r	e
o	x	w	w	v
u	f	y	f	e
r	c	h	q	r
w	a	n	t	y

Complete the story with the words you found.

George and the man _____
at the movies.

"What do you _____
to eat, George?"

George chooses popcorn
_____ time!

"Here is _____ popcorn,"
says the boy at the snack bar.

Pop! Pop! Pop!

George has five pieces of popcorn.
Count the popcorn in each group.
Write the numbers.

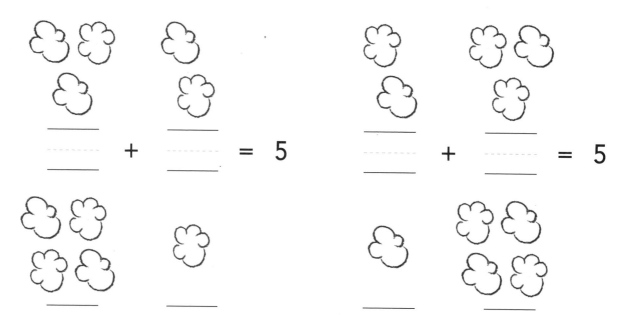

_____ + _____ = 5   _____ + _____ = 5

_____ + _____ = 5   _____ + _____ = 5

Pass the Popcorn

George takes a handful of popcorn.
Write how many pieces he has. Then draw a line
to the bucket with the same number.

$$\begin{array}{r} 1 \\ +\ 4 \\ \hline \end{array}$$

$$\begin{array}{r} 5 \\ +\ 2 \\ \hline \end{array}$$

$$\begin{array}{r} 3 \\ +\ 4 \\ \hline \end{array}$$

$$\begin{array}{r} 4 \\ +\ 2 \\ \hline \end{array}$$

$$\begin{array}{r} 3 \\ +\ 3 \\ \hline \end{array}$$

$$\begin{array}{r} 2 \\ +\ 3 \\ \hline \end{array}$$

A Busy Day

George has a busy day. Look at the **hour hand**.
Write the time.

It is ___7:00___.

George wakes up.

It is _____.

George plays with his toys.

It is _____.

George eats lunch.

It is _____.

George goes to the movies.

George eats
dinner at 6:00.
Trace the hour hand.

George goes to bed
one hour later.
Draw the hour hand.

Run George, Run!

Write the time shown on the clock.
Is George late? Circle **yes** or **no**.

The picnic starts at 1:00.

It is _____.   Is George late?

yes   **no**

The movie starts at 3:00.

It is _____.   Is George late?

yes   **no**

The circus starts at 4:00.

It is _____.   Is George late?

yes   **no**

The race starts at 11:00.

It is _____.   Is George late?

yes   **no**

Hand Shadows

George is at
the movies.
It is dark.
Then the movie starts.

Look at the picture.
Circle where the light
comes from.

George blocks the light with his hands.
Which shadow
did he make?
Draw a line.

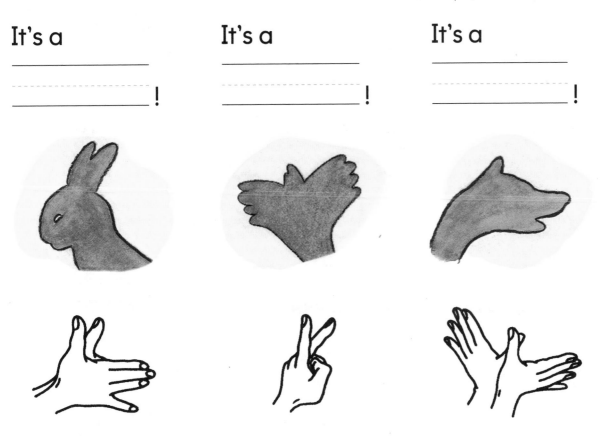

George can make a **bird**, a **dog**, and a **rabbit**.
Write the name of each animal shadow.
Then draw a line to the hands that match.

It's a
_____
_____ !

It's a
_____
_____ !

It's a
_____
_____ !

Now who is blocking the light? Draw him.

How Do You Feel?

A movie can make you feel **happy**, **sad**, **angry**, or **scared**.
Use these words to describe how George feels.

George feels . . .

_____   _____   _____   _____

What is George watching? Draw it.

You did it!

Make an **X** next to things you know.

Place a sticker

- [ ] I know that stories about real life have **facts**.

- [ ] I know that made-up stories are **fiction**.

- [ ] I can add **–s** or **–es** to a word to show more than one.

- [ ] I can use the word **is** to describe what George **is** doing.

- [ ] I can use the word **are** to describe what George and the man **are** doing.

- [ ] I know that **2 + 3** and **3 + 2** have the same answer.

- [ ] I can tell time in **hours** and **half hours**.

- [ ] I know that a movie projector makes **light**.

- [ ] I can make a **shadow** by blocking light.

- [ ] I can feel happy, sad, angry, or scared.

Turn the page to start a new adventure!

93

Hospital

George is curious about . . .

 **Reading**   syllables; identifying story problems; high-frequency words

 **Math**   adding to solve word problems; 10 more and 10 less

 **Science**   properties of matter

 **Social and Emotional**   caring for others

George Volunteers

One day the man with the yellow hat took George to the hospital. George was curious. He was not sick or hurt.

"We are going to visit the children staying here," said the man.
"We can help them feel better."

George wondered how he could help.
He was not a doctor. He was not a nurse.
He was just a little monkey.

A nurse greeted them. She brought them
to a playroom. "Can you play with the
children, George?" she asked.

 A volunteer is someone who helps. How can George help the
children? Who would you like to help?

George loved to play!
He found a box of puppets.
He put two on his arms
and two on his legs.

He wiggled them in the air.
The children laughed.

George looked for something else to do.
He saw an empty chair with wheels.
He climbed in.

The chair
started to
go, go, go!
A nurse shouted,
"Oh no! Oh no!"

Why do you think George could not stop the chair?
What are some things you *should* and *should not* do in a hospital?

George saw a group of people.
He tried to slow down, but the chair
was going too fast!

CRASH!

The chair stopped,
but George kept going!
The children watched him
fly through the air.
When George landed, he hurt his ankle.

The doctor examined it.
The nurse put ice on it.
Brr! The ice was cold,
but George felt
a *little* better.

Later, a friend from the playroom
stopped by. "I never saw a flying monkey,"
said the boy.

George smiled.
Soon he forgot
about his ankle.
He felt *much* better.
It was nice to have a friend at the hospital.

How did the boy make George feel better?
What makes you feel better when you are hurt?

Clap to It!

Clap to count the number of beats.
Say each word. Then write the number.

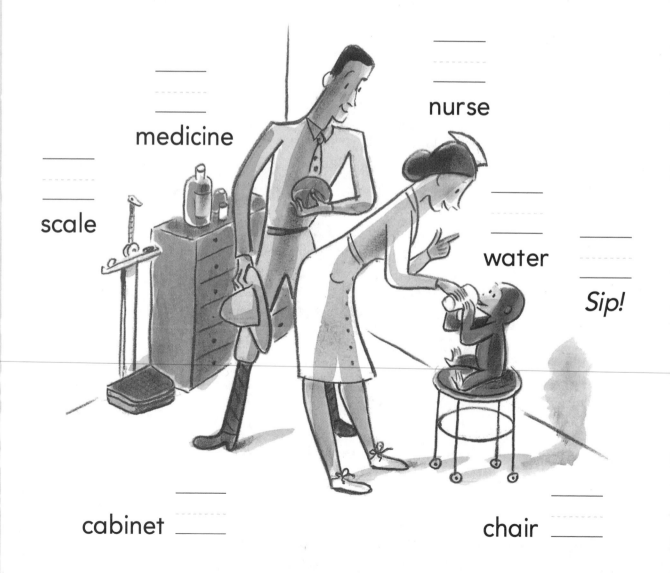

wheel

___1___ beat

wheelchair

___2___ beats

___ ___

medicine

___ ___

scale

nurse

___ ___

water

___ ___

Sip!

___ ___

cabinet ___

chair ___

In the Playroom

Say each word.

Draw a line under words with one beat.

Draw two lines under words with two beats.

table

book

chair

paint

wagon

puppets

Can you find something that has four beats?
Circle it!

There's a Problem

Look at the picture. Who knows that there is a problem? Circle them.

Circle the picture that shows the problem.

What's Wrong, George?

Tell what is wrong with George.
Choose the best word to complete
each sentence.

George's _____ hurts.

  foot   tummy

He feels _____.

  angry   sick

He does not want to _____.

  eat   read

Circle the picture that can explain
why George has a tummy ache.
Then write to tell what happened.

_____

George _____

_____!

Doctor Visit

George went to the doctor.
Choose the best word
to complete each sentence.

The man with the yellow hat took
_____

George _____ the doctor.

     with   to

    _____

"George _____ not eat," the man said.

    was   will

The doctor looked _____ George's throat.

    down   there

_____ he felt George's tummy.

Then   When

"George _____ need an X-ray," said the doctor.

    may   made

"An X-ray is a picture of _____ insides."

    your   their

The Missing Piece!

Write the missing piece in each sentence.

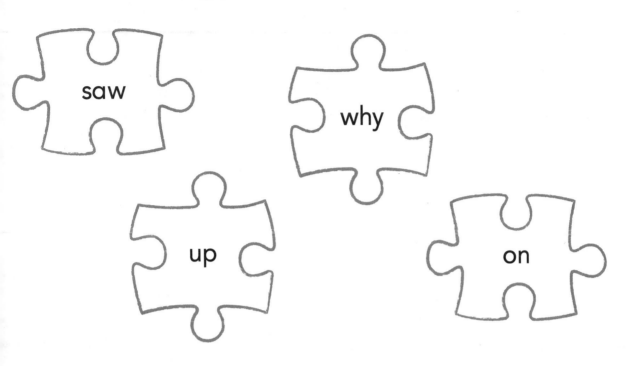

saw

why

up

on

George climbed _____ on the table.

The doctor turned _____ the X-ray machine.

The man with the yellow hat
_____ a puzzle piece.

Now they knew
_____ George
felt sick.

Puppet Show

George puts on a puppet show for the children.

George has 4 puppets. There are 7 more in the box. How many puppets are there in all?

___4___ + ___7___ = _____ _____ puppets

There are 11 puppets. George brings in 5 more from home. How many puppets are there now?

_____ + _____ = _____ _____ puppets

10 children hold a puppet in their right hand. 4 children hold a puppet in their left hand. How many puppets are there in all?

_____ + _____ = _____ _____ puppets

Draw a new hand puppet on George's arm.

108

Balloon Animals

A clown visits the hospital.
He makes balloon animals for the children.

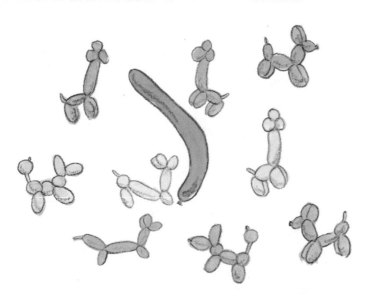

He makes 7 red giraffes and 9 blue giraffes.
How many balloon giraffes are there?

7 + 9 = _____ giraffes

He makes 9 blue dogs and 6 green dogs.
How many balloon dogs are there?

_____ + _____ = _____ dogs

He gives balloons to 8 boys and 7 girls.
How many children have balloon animals?

_____ + _____ = _____ children

109

Balloons

Help George count the balloons. Find 10 less and 10 more than the middle number.

10 less		10 more
_____	11	21
_____	14	_____
_____	29	_____
_____	12	_____
_____	26	_____

110

Flowers

Now help George count the flowers in the gift shop. Find 10 less or 10 more to fill in the blanks.

10 less			10 more
1	_____ 		_____
3	_____		_____
_____	_____		30
_____	34		_____
_____	104		_____

Show 10 less. Make an **X** on 10 flowers.

There are _____ flowers left.

Twenty Questions

Write one word that tells about both pictures.

Both are _crunchy_.

Both are _____.

Both are _____.

Both are _____.

George is thinking of a picture on this page.
It is hard and yellow.
Can you figure out what it is?

It is a _____.

Now ask a friend to think of a picture
on this page. Ask **yes** or **no** questions about
how it looks, feels, sounds, or tastes.
Can you guess what it is?

Are You Okay?

George fell down! What will you say to him? Write it.

_____

- -

_____

Don't be sad.   Are you hurt?   It will be okay.

Circle things that can make George feel better.

a hug

George's teddy

balloons

George is upset.
Make a silly face
to cheer him up!

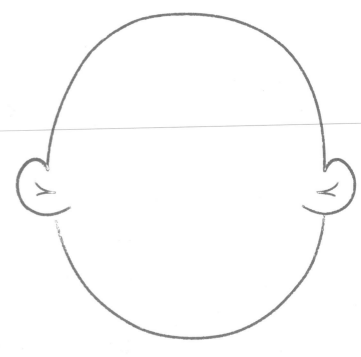

You did it!

Make an X next to things you know.

Place a sticker

☐ I can count the **syllables** in a word by clapping. Wheelchair has two syllables.

☐ I can tell the **problem** in a story.

☐ I know the words **to**, **will**, **down**, and **then** on sight.

☐ I can add to solve some **word problems**.

☐ I can find **10 less** and **10 more** than a number.

☐ I can tell how something **looks** or **feels**. These are **properties**.

☐ George's properties are brown and hairy!

☐ I can ask, "Are you okay?" to show that I care.

Turn the page to start a new adventure!

Recycling

George is curious about . . .

 **Reading** order of events; character traits; high-frequency words

 **Math** classifying objects; picture and bar graphs

 **Science** caring for the environment; transparent objects

 **Social and Emotional** being a good citizen

Good As New

George built a tower out of paper and boxes.
It was taller than George. Maybe it was taller
than the man with the yellow hat!

The man brought more things to add to the tower. "We can recycle these, too," he told George.

"Then they can be turned into something new." George loved new things!

What are paper and boxes made from?
Name three paper products that you use every day.

119

So he recycled all afternoon.
He turned paper into
something new.

Paper airplanes!

He turned a banana peel
into something new.

A hat!

He turned paper clips
into a necklace.

He turned toothpaste into paint!

It was fun to recycle!

"George!" cried the man. "What are
you doing?" George wondered if he
recycled the wrong way.

George tried to recycle toothpaste. Can toothpaste be recycled?
Paper can be recycled. What other materials can be recycled?

The next day, the man took George to the Science Museum. "We can learn how to recycle here," he said.

Inside, George saw a red bin filled with paper. He saw a yellow bin filled with bottles and cans.

George learned that it was his job to put paper, bottles, and cans into special bins. Then it was someone else's job to make them into something new.

Now George knew how to take care of his planet!

Can shoes be recycled, or turned into something new?
Can shoes be reused by someone else? What else can be reused?

Easy As 1, 2, 3

George learned how to recycle.
Write **1**, **2**, and **3** to put the story in order.

Tell how to recycle a bottle.
Write **1**, **2**, and **3** to put the steps in order.

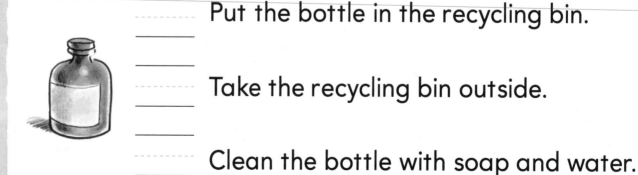

_____ Put the bottle in the recycling bin.

_____ Take the recycling bin outside.

_____ Clean the bottle with soap and water.

Reduce, Reuse, Recycle

Draw a line from each word to its definition.

reduce   use something again

reuse   use less of something

recycle   use old things to make new things

Now use the words to label each picture.

off

_____
reuse

_____
reduce

Circle what the paper can be made into.

_____
recycle

About Him, About Her

Read each description.
Draw a line to the picture that matches.

He is funny.
He makes George laugh.

He is curious. He likes to
be helpful. Sometimes he
makes a mess!

He is smart and kind.
He helps children learn.

She is brave. She helps
keep people safe.

George Is . . .

Read each sentence.
Circle the word that describes George.

George waters the plant.

caring   mean

George observes the butterfly.

noisy   curious

George picks up trash.

helpful   lazy

George tries on the man's hat.

afraid   silly

Write two words to describe yourself.

_____   _____

I am _____ and _____ .

Old Tire, New Swing

The man made a surprise for George.
Choose the best word to complete each sentence.

The man _____ home.

came   have

He _____ an old tire.

had   made

He tied a _____ rope to it.

little   long

He threw the rope _____ a branch.

before   over

George jumped onto _____ new swing.

him   his

Whee!

128

Green Day

George went to the park.
Circle the best word to complete each sentence.

It (**can** / **was**) Green Day at the park.

The (**number** / **people**) planted trees.

First, (**there** / **they**) dug a hole.

Next, they (**down** / **put**) the tree into it.

Then, they filled the hole (**will** / **with**) soil.

Last, someone gave the tree (**water** / **words**).

Circle who is doing the first step.

Reuse or Recycle?

Can each item be reused or recycled?
Add it to the correct list.

reuse

recycle

_____

_____

_____

_____

carton

shoes

box

hat

can

toy

Reuse this jar. Draw
something new in it.

Turn Food into Soil

Some people don't throw away food.
They **compost** it. That turns food into soil.
Circle foods.

Can Collection

George collected cans to recycle.

Thursday	🥫 🥫 🥫 🥫
Friday	🥫 🥫 🥫 🥫 🥫 🥫 🥫
Saturday	🥫 🥫 🥫 🥫 🥫 🥫 🥫 🥫

He collected _____ cans on Thursday.

He collected _____ cans on Friday.

He collected _____ cans in all.

He collected the most cans on _____.

George collected 3 fewer cans
on Sunday than on Saturday.
Draw how many cans he
collected on Sunday.

Paper, Bottles, and Cans

Color a square for each item George collected.

4   2   3

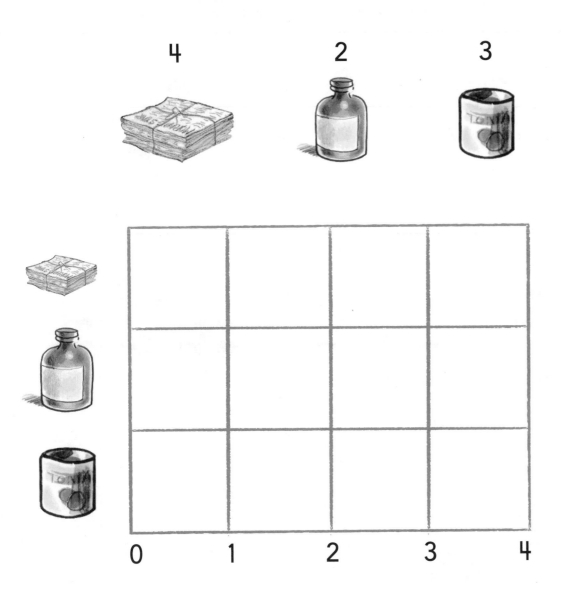

0   1   2   3   4

133

Keep It Clean

George helps keep land, water, and air clean.
Write **land**, **water**, or **air** to tell how.

George picks up trash.
_____

This keeps the _____ clean.

George rides a bike.
_____

This keeps the _____ clean.

George takes his toys home
from the beach.
_____

This keeps the _____ clean.

George plants a tree.
_____

This keeps the _____ clean.

Draw a line to complete each sentence.

If you pollute . . .

then there will be **trash on the ground**.

If you litter . . .

then you can help **turn old things into new things**.

If you pick up trash . . .

then the **air and water will be dirty**.

If you recycle . . .

then you can help **keep the planet clean** for people, plants, and animals.

Living things need a clean planet to be healthy. Circle ten living things. (Maybe you can find more!)

Is It See-Through?

The man can see through his eyeglasses. They are **transparent**.

Circle things that are transparent. Cross out things that are not transparent.

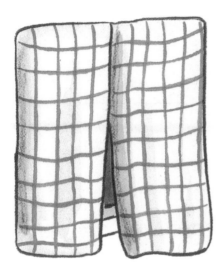

Circle the transparent
parts on the bus.

137

Being a Good Citizen

Do the Right Thing

Read some ways that George is a good citizen.
Color in the star next to things you do too.

George asks for help when he needs it.

 I do too.

George tells the truth, even if it is difficult.

 I do too.

George takes care of the environment.

 I do too.

George takes care of the environment
by making less trash. Color in the star
above things you do too.

George reuses   George uses   George
shopping bags.   both sides of   donates his
                    the paper.   old books.

138

You did it!

Make an **X** next to things you know.

Place a sticker

☐ I can retell a story's events in order.

☐ I learned the new words **reduce**, **reuse**, and **recycle**.

☐ I can describe George as **curious** and **helpful**.

☐ I can read the words **came**, **long**, **over**, **people**, and **water** on sight.

☐ I can **sort** objects to be **reused**, **recycled**, or **composted**.

☐ I can read and make a **graph**.

☐ I know how to keep land, air, and water clean.

☐ I can see through **transparent** things.

☐ I know that a **good citizen** is caring.

Turn the page to start a new adventure!

Vacation

George is curious about . . .

Reading   proper nouns; commands; questions; suffixes; contractions

Math   solving word problems; equal and not equal; adding tens; math facts

Science   the daytime sky, the nighttime sky

Social and Emotional   making good choices

A Road Trip

George and his friend
were taking a trip.
They were going
to see a landmark.
That's an important place.

This landmark was far away.
They needed a map to find it.
The man pointed to a shape on the map.
"That's where we're going," he said.

The place was
called South Dakota.
George wondered
what was there.

The farther they drove,
the more things
looked different.
The buildings started out
tall and got shorter.

The trees
started out short
and got taller!

South Dakota is a state. What state do you live in?
Do you find tall buildings in the city or the country?

They drove past a herd of cows.
Moo, called the mamas to their babies.
Then a train appeared.
It raced alongside the car.

George counted
the cars on the train.
Chuh-chug.
Chuh-chug.
Chuh-chug.
Then it was gone.

The man kept driving.

Sometimes George would close his eyes.
When he opened them,
the landscape changed again.
This time, he saw hot air balloons
float up into the sky.

The man stopped
the car for a short time . . .

. . . then he kept driving.

What did George see on his road trip?
How do you know this was a long road trip?

"Wake up, George!"
said the man. "We're in
South Dakota!"
George opened his eyes.

The man led him to a huge patio.
George saw the landmark. Someone
had carved the faces of four presidents
into a mountain—Mount Rushmore.

It was the largest artwork
George had ever seen. *Click.*
George and the man smiled for a picture.

After several days, it was time to go home.
George could see the landmark for many miles.

And when he could
no longer see it,
he looked at his
picture and smiled.

 Why was George able to see the landmark for many miles?
George had a souvenir to remember the trip. What was it?

Mount Rushmore

A **proper noun** names a special person, animal, or place. It begins with a capital letter. Circle each proper noun. Then write it correctly.

There is (george.) _George_

He is going to south dakota.

_____

_____

He is visiting mount rushmore.

_____

_____

The face of george washington
is carved into the mountain.

_____

_____

George and the man
visit Mount Rushmore.
Name a special place
that you want to visit.

_____

I want to visit _____.

148

The Scott Family

Sometimes there is a **title** before a person's name.
It begins with a capital letter.
Draw a line under each title.
Then write the title and name correctly.

mr. scott

_____

_____

mrs. scott

_____

_____

Circle the proper nouns in each sentence.

The Scott family takes a trip across the country.

Mr. and Mrs. Scott take turns driving.

Jim and Lucy sit in the back seat.

Write a proper noun to tell who will
take care of Lucy's fish Golda.

_____ will!

Find George!

A **command** is a sentence that tells someone to do something. Draw a line under the commands.

Be careful.   George climbs.   Look over there.

Write a command. Tell George what to do.

_____

- -

_____ .

Now circle the command that shows strong feeling.

Climb down, George.

Climb down, George!

150

Where Is George?

A **question** is a sentence that asks something.
Write the correct word to begin each sentence.
Write the correct end mark.

Can   What   Where   Who   Why

_____ is George going ?

_____ is George holding onto the pole __

_____ is looking at George __

_____ you see the man with the yellow hat __

_____ is he doing __

Big City

George and the man took a carriage ride. Add the correct suffix to each word.

–y   **–ly**   **–ful**

It was a snow_____ day.

Snowflakes fell soft_____.

It was peace_____.

The horse moved slow_____.

George felt joy_____.

Why do you think George felt joyful?

_____

_____

What's Up, George?

George is at the museum.
Write a **contraction** for the underlined words.

can't   He's   isn't   It's   There's

He <u>is</u> looking for the man.
_____
_____

George <u>cannot</u> see him.
_____
_____

The man <u>is not</u> below.
_____
_____

<u>There is</u> the man!
_____
_____

The man says,
"<u>It is</u> time to go home."
_____
_____

Goodbye, Big City!

Road Trip Math

Read each word problem.
How will you solve it?
Circle **add** or **subtract**.
Then write a number sentence.

George has 15 crackers. He eats 6 crackers.
How many crackers are left?

add   subtract

15 $-$ 6 = 9 crackers

George sees 5 mama cows and 7 baby cows.
How many cows does George see?

add   subtract

_____ ◯ _____ = _____ cows

George sees 9 hot air balloons. 3 float away.
How many balloons are left?

add   subtract

_____ ◯ _____ = _____ balloons

Big City Math

Read each word problem.
How will you solve it?
Circle **add** or **subtract**.
Then write a number sentence.

George saw 20 cabs. 5 were empty.
How many cabs had riders?

add   **subtract**

____ ◯ ____ = ____ cabs

5 people get into a cab. 3 more get in.
How many riders are in the cab?

add   **subtract**

____ ◯ ____ = ____ riders

11 people get on the elevator.
3 people get off.
2 more people get on.
How many people are on
the elevator now?

____ ◯ ____ ◯ ____ = ____ people

Set Sail

George and the man set sail.
Help them stay on course.

The symbol = means
the same as.

Is this true? $3 + 3 = 6 - 0$

$3 + 3 = $ **6** and $6 - 0 = $ **6**.

6 is the same as 6. *It is true.*

Which is **true**? Circle it.
Which is **false**? Cross it out.

$7 + 4 = 6 + 6$	$5 + 5 = 8 + 2$
$7 - 1 = 9 - 3$	$13 - 6 = 9 - 4$
$6 + 4 = 1 + 9$	$9 - 2 = 2 + 9$
$12 - 2 = 13 - 5$	$4 + 3 = 1 + 6$
$14 - 7 = 10 - 3$	$9 - 4 = 8 - 1$
$0 + 7 = 5 + 3$	$6 + 9 = 7 + 8$

George sets sail in the sky. Find him.

Draw a path from the hat to George.
Follow the clues.

1. Go to 10 + 10 + 10 + 7.

2. Go to 20 + 3.

3. Go to 20 + 20 + 4.

4. Go to 10 + 30 + 10 + 7.

5. Go to 10 + 20 + 40 + 8.

6. Go to 30 + 10 + 30 +5.

7. Go to 10 + 10 + 2.

8. Circle the balloon with George.

157

Family Vacation

George and the man are a family.
They go on vacation together.
Numbers have families, too.

Use the numbers in each family to make facts.

$6 + 4 = 10$ $10 - 4 = 6$

$4 + 6 = 10$ $10 - 6 = 4$

_____ $+ 7 = 8$ $8 -$ _____ $= 1$

$7 + 1 = 8$ _____ $- 1 = 7$

$5 +$ _____ $= 8$ _____ $- 3 = 5$

$3 + 5 = 8$ $8 -$ _____ $= 3$

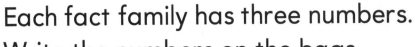

Each fact family has three numbers.
Write the numbers on the bags.
Then add or subtract to make facts.

$5 + \underline{\quad} = 7$ $\underline{\quad} - 5 = 2$

$2 + 5 = \underline{\quad}$ $\underline{\quad} - \underline{\quad} = \underline{\quad}$

$\underline{\quad} + 8 = 10$ $10 - 2 = \underline{\quad}$

$\underline{\quad} + 2 = 10$ $\underline{\quad} - \underline{\quad} = \underline{\quad}$

$\underline{\quad} + 6 = 9$ $9 - \underline{\quad} = 6$

$6 + 3 = \underline{\quad}$ $\underline{\quad} - \underline{\quad} = \underline{\quad}$

Math Facts

Daytime Sky

George looks up at the daytime sky.
Draw what is in the daytime sky.

Use the words to tell about the sun.

clouds   **heat**   **light**   **star**

The sun is the closest _____ to Earth.

The sun gives _____ and _____ to Earth.

Now it is raining.
Where did the sun go?

It is hidden behind the _____.

Nighttime Sky

George looks up at the nighttime sky.
What else is in the nighttime sky? Draw it.

Use the words to tell about the moon.

light   **moon**   **rock**   **telescope**

_____

George uses a _____ to look
at the sky.

_____

It makes the _____ look bigger.

_____

The moon is a ball of _____.

_____

It does not give off its own _____.
It reflects the sun's light.

Have a Safe Trip!

Tell George how to stay safe on a trip.
Make an **X** next to what you would do.

If I am in a car . . .

☐ I wear a seatbelt.　　☐ I do not wear a seatbelt.

If I am in a boat . . .

☐ I wear a life jacket.　　☐ I sit on my life jacket.

If I want to see something new . . .

☐ I walk away from my family.

☐ I stay with my family.

☐ I never go with people who say
they know my family.

Draw a
life jacket
on George.

Then draw
yourself on
the boat.

You did it!

Make an X next to things you know.

Place a sticker

☐ I know that a **proper noun** names a special person or place. It begins with a capital letter.

☐ A **command** is a sentence that tells someone to do something.

☐ A **question** is a sentence that asks something.

☐ I can use an apostrophe to push two words together. **It's** easy.

☐ I can turn a word problem into a number sentence.

☐ I know that **=** means **the same as**.

☐ I can make **facts** about **number families**.

☐ I know the **sun** gives light and heat to Earth.

☐ I know the **moon** does not give light.

☐ I can make good choices.

Turn the page to start a new adventure!

Hiking

George is curious about . . .

Reading   inflectional endings –ing
and –ed; prepositions;
high-frequency words

Math   measuring with nonstandard
units; adding tens;
subtracting tens

Science   environment;
interdependence
of living things

**Social and
Emotional**   following rules

George Goes on a Hike

George and the man
with the yellow hat
went hiking
in the woods.
They followed a path.

"Stay on the trail, George," said the man.
"Then you won't get lost!"

George wondered what kinds
of animals lived in the woods.
Just then, he heard a noise.
It came from behind a bush.

What could it be?

An alligator?

A hippo?

A lion?

George was curious.
He wanted to find out!

Which animals on this page do not live in the woods?
What do you think is behind the bush?

167

George crept toward the bush.
He saw a feather
on the ground.
It was soft
and blue.

George peeked
behind the bush.
There was a blue bird.
It plucked a worm out
of a hole and flew away.
George stepped off
the trail to follow it.

The bird flew
up and up,
into a tree.
George climbed
up and up, too.

Chirp! George saw a nest.
Inside, a baby bird sat and
waited for its mama.

And here she was!
The mama bird
fed the worm
to the hatchling.

Baby birds, alligators, and turtles are called *hatchlings*.
Can you guess why? Living things grow and change.
How will the hatchling grow and change?

George climbed down. He was excited
to tell his friend what he saw.

But he could not find the trail. He was lost!
So George did what the baby bird did.
He sat and waited.

And sure enough, his friend
came back to find him!

What does George keep from his hike?
Did you ever find something interesting on a hike? What was it?

171

What Is Happening?

Tell what is happening on George's hike.
Add **–ing** to each word.

chirp___ing___   creep_____   fly_____   wait_____

Now write each new word in a sentence.

George is
_____
_____.

The bird is _____.

The baby bird is _____.

George is _____
for the man.

172

What Happened?

Tell what happened on George's hike.
Add **-ed** to each word.

climb_ed____   peek_____   pick_____   walk_____

Now write each new word in a sentence.

George _____   George _____
in the woods.   up a feather.

George _____   George _____
behind a bush.   a tree.

What did you think was behind the bush?
Draw it. Then complete the sentence.

I guess_____ that it was a _____.

173

Home Sweet Home

Many animals live in the woods.
Use these words to tell what you see.

above   **between**   **in**   **on**   **under**

A raccoon sits _____ a rock.

A stream runs _____ the trees.

Fish jump _____ the stream.

A skunk hides _____ a bush.

The birds sit on a branch _____
the ground.

174

Where Is George?

Follow the directions to show where George is.

☐   Draw a tree **behind** George.

☐   Draw a squirrel going **up** the tree.

☐   Draw a bird **above** George.

☐   Draw a rabbit **beside** George.

Describe your drawing. Complete each sentence.

George is _____ the woods.

on   in

He is surrounded _____ friends!

by   to

175

A Hiking Hippo

Unscramble each word. Then write it in the sentence to complete the story.

George and the man took a walk _____ the woods.
ni

"Look _____ there!" said the man.
vero

George _____ a hippo on the trail.
aws

"This is _____ strange," said the man.
ryve

"Why is _____ a hippo on the trail?"
heter

So it _____ not get lost!
illw

176

A Walk in the Rain

Find these words in the puzzle.

big　**had**　**one**　**walk**　**want**　**was**

o　t　a　h　a　d

n　n　v　l　z　g

e　a　e　t　a　g

s　w　a　l　k　w

b　i　g　b　s　a

p　l　c　u　j　s

Now complete the story with the words you found.

_____

It _____ raining.

_____

George went for a _____.

_____　_____

He _____ a _____ umbrella.

_____

George did not _____ to get wet.

_____

No _____ got wet!

177

Feather Measure

Use the feather to measure.

about _____

about _____

about _____

about _____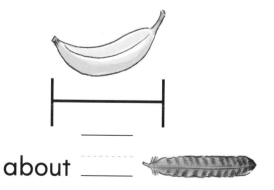

George sees a  red worm.

The red worm is about 1  long.

—————

Draw a blue worm that is about 3  long.

Draw an orange worm that is about 1  longer than the red worm.

The _____ worm is the **shortest** worm.

The _____ worm is the **longest** worm.

Pack a Snack

George and the man pack snacks for the hike.

Each  = 1 ten

Draw bags to show how many tens there are.
Add the tens. Then write a number sentence.

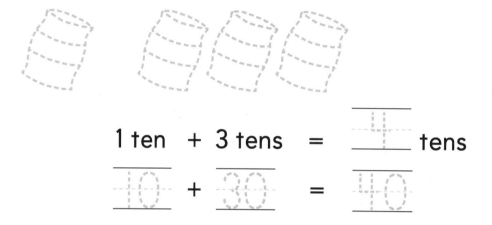

1 ten + 3 tens = 4 tens

10 + 30 = 40

3 tens + 2 tens = _____ tens

30 + 20 =

4 tens + 3 tens = _____ tens

40 + 30 =

George and the man give away snacks.

Cross out bags to show how many tens they give away. Subtract the tens. Then write a number sentence.

6 tens – 4 tens = __2__ tens

60 – 40 = 20

7 tens – 4 tens = _____ tens

70 – 40 = ___

5 tens – 2 tens = _____ tens

50 – 20 = ___

Environments

Up, Down, All Around

The bird lives in the woods. That is where it can get what it needs to survive.

It needs **food**.   It needs **shelter**.

Write one thing each animal needs.
Can it find what it needs in the woods?
Circle **yes** or **no**.

It needs: Is this in the woods?

   bugs   yes   no

yes   no

yes   no

182

I Need You!

Animals need plants for food and shelter.
Label each picture. Is it **food** or **shelter**?

_____
- - - - - - - - - -
_____

_____
- - - - - - - - - -
_____

Plants need animals, too.
A squirrel will bury nuts to eat later.
Some of these nuts will grow into trees.
Where can a tree grow? Draw it.

A Walk in the Woods

George goes on a hike. Color in the leaf next to things George should do.

Walk with a friend.

Pet the animals.

Feed the animals.

Watch the animals from a distance.

Can George take it home? Write **Yes** or **No**.

_____

_____, George.

_____

_____, George.

_____

_____, George.

You did it!

Make an **X** next to things you know.

Place a sticker

☐ I can add **–ing** to some words to tell what is happening now.

☐ I can add **–ed** to some words to tell what happened in the past.

☐ I can tell where something is by using **on**, **under**, or **above**.

☐ I know the words **in**, **over**, **very**, and **was** on sight.

☐ I can measure with **nonstandard units**.

☐ I can **add** and **subtract tens**.

☐ I know that animals need **food** and **shelter**. They live in places where these needs are met.

☐ I know that plants and animals need each other.

☐ I know how to keep animals safe when I am hiking through their home.

Turn the page to start a new adventure!

Pizza

George is curious about . . .

Reading   conjunctions; shades of meaning; adjectives; high-frequency words

Math   equal parts; halves and fourths; drawing and writing the time

Science   natural resources: plants and animals; measuring tool

Social and Emotional   apologizing

It's a Party!

George flipped with excitement!
He was invited to a party.
He wondered what kind of party it would be.

A birthday party?

A costume party?

A dance party?

Maybe it was a
slumber party! *Zzz.*

What is George doing at the slumber party?
What do you think *slumber* means?

189

On the day of the party, George arrived at his friend's house. She put a puffy white hat on his head. She tied an apron around his waist. "Welcome to my pizza party!" she said.

A pizza party! George cheered. The girl's mother gave each child a ball of dough.

George used a rolling pin to make it flat.

George rolled the dough this way and that way.

George rolled the dough right off the table!

Now it was too big to fit in the oven. George had an idea! He cut the dough into small shapes.

What tool does George use to make the dough flat?
What can you make out of dough?

191

The children spooned sauce
onto the dough. They added cheese
and toppings.

Then it was time to bake the pizzas.

When they came out of the oven, they did not look quite like pizzas. They looked better! And they tasted . . .

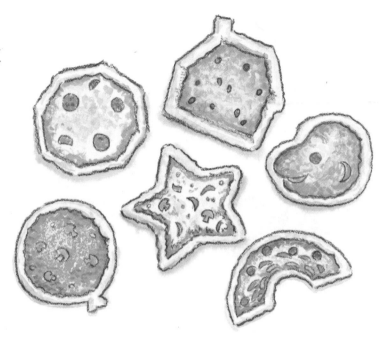

Yum! everyone said.

Which pizza has ten sides? Which pizza has no sides?
Which pizza looks like a stop sign?

Conjunctions

Pepperoni, Please!

Which toppings does each child want?
Trace the joining words to find out.
Then circle the toppings.

 wants mushrooms and sauce.

 mushrooms   pepperoni   peppers   sauce

 wants mushrooms or pepperoni.

 mushrooms   pepperoni   peppers   sauce

 wants peppers and pepperoni. Draw it.

 mushrooms

 peppers

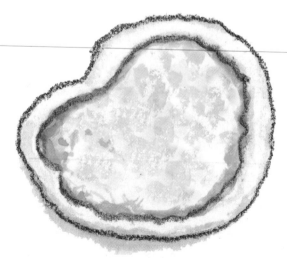

 pepperoni

 sauce

194

Super Star Pizza

What toppings do you like on your pizza?
Write them below.

I like _____ and _____ .

I like _____ but I don't

like _____ .

Draw toppings on your pizza.
Then tell about your pizza.

My pizza has _____ and _____

but it does not have _____ .

The Best Word

Which word describes the picture better?
Write it.

_____

The dough is _____.

       big   huge

_____

The kitchen is _____.

     crowded   messy

_____

The girl's mother is _____.

      upset   scared

Pizza Is . . .

One word does not fit. Cross it out.

Pizza is _____.

chewy

soft

sweet

Draw a line to connect words that almost mean the same thing.

warm   cold

yummy   hot

cool   tasty

Circle one word above. Use it in a sentence.

_____

_____

_____

_____ .

Chef George

George is a pizza chef. Write the correct words to tell how Chef George makes pizza.

catch   first   them   up   will   with

The _____ step is to make the dough. You

_____ need water and flour. Mix _____.

You can roll the dough _____ a rolling pin.

Or you can toss it _____ in the air.

Do not forget to _____ it!

How will you __make__ the dough? Circle one.

Roll it!

Toss it!

into   **over**   **some**

time   **too**   **your**

Next, add _____ tomato sauce. Sprinkle cheese

_____ the sauce. Then add _____ favorite

toppings. It is _____ to bake the pizza. The oven

is _____ hot for Chef George! He asks a friend

to put the pizza _____ the oven.

What is the last step? Put the words in the right
order to find out!

down   **and**   **eat**   **Sit**

_____

_____

Pizza Night

George and the man share a pizza.
Circle pizzas that show **two equal parts**, or halves.

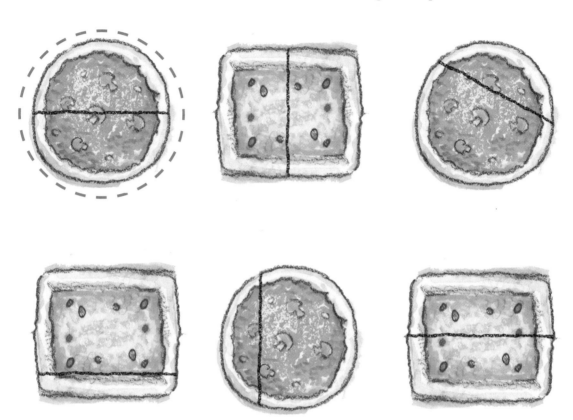

Cut each pizza once more to make
four equal parts, or fourths.

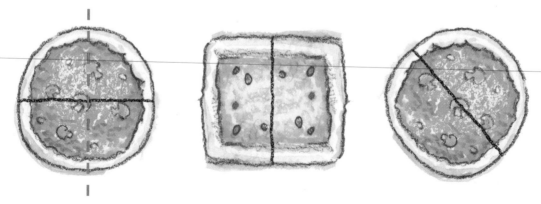

Pizza Delivery

Which pizza did each person order? Circle it.

 Cut my pizza into ___halves___.

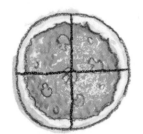 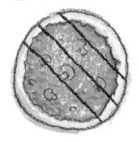

 Cut my pizza into ___fourths___.

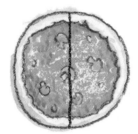 

 Cut my pizza into ___quarters___.

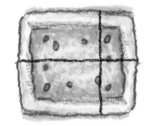 

Add pepperoni to ___half of___ my pizza.

Pizza Time

George and the man order a pizza.
It arrives a half hour later.

It is _5:00_.
The hour hand points to 5.
The minute hand points to 12.
Trace the minute hand.

Now it is _5:30_.
The hour hand points
between 5 and 6.
The minute hand points to 6.
Trace the minute hand.

Look at the hour hand on each clock.
Write the time. Draw the minute hand.

There goes the pizza delivery van!
When will the next pizza get delivered?
Look for the pattern.
Circle the clock that comes next.

Food for Thought

Plants and animals are natural resources.
We use them for food.
Draw a line from the plant or animal to
how we use it.

cow's milk

tomato sauce

tomatoes

cheese

hen

orange juice

orange

eggs

Circle two natural resources
George used to make pizza.

One Pizza, Two Pizzas

George needs these ingredients to make one pizza.

 =

1 cup water   1 cup flour   1 cup sauce

Circle how many George needs to make **2** s.

Circle how many George needs to make **3** s.

Circle how many George needs to make **4** s.

George used all the ingredients below.

He made _____ s.

George Makes a Mess!

"Look at this mess!" said the girl's mom.

Trace what George should say.

I did not do it .   I am sorry .

Circle what George should do.

Clean up, George.   Run away, George!

Did you ever spill something? What did you say?

_____

_____

_____

You did it!

Make an **X** next to things you know.

Place a sticker

- ☐ I know when to use the joining words **and**, **or**, and **but**.

- ☐ I know that **big** and **huge** are almost the same.

- ☐ I can read the words **catch**, **first**, and **them** without sounding them out.

- ☐ I can cut a pizza into **two equal parts**, or **halves**.

- ☐ I can cut pizza into **four equal parts**, or **fourths**.

- ☐ I can tell time to the **hour** and **half hour**.

- ☐ I know that food comes from **plants** and **animals**.

- ☐ I can measure with a **measuring cup**.

- ☐ I can say *I am sorry* if I spill something.

Turn the page to start a new adventure!

Jobs

George is curious about . . .

Reading   isolating sounds; initial and final sounds; the narrator

Math   different ways to make ten; using the associative property to add

Science   water; natural and human-made materials

Social and Emotional   helping at home

A Job for George

The man with the yellow hat was going to work. "Have a good day, George!" He waved goodbye. George wanted to go to work, too.

George saw people going to work on a bus.
He rode along.

The bus stopped downtown. The people got off. Some went to work in offices. Others went to work in stores.

Some people take the bus to work. How else do people go to work?
What is a job that someone can do inside? Outside?

George saw a restaurant
with a help wanted sign.
Mmm. George liked food.
Maybe he could help.

George went inside.

A man in a hat and apron
turned to look at George.
"Hello," he said. "I am the
chef. You must be here for
the job. Let's get to work!"

The chef showed George a sink filled with dirty dishes. George washed, dried, and stacked them. "Good work!" said the chef.

George looked for more things to do. He saw a big shiny pot. It was filled with noodles. George tasted them.

"Oh no!" said the chef. "You cannot eat the food. This is not the job for you!"

Where does a chef work? What kind of work does a chef do? What did George do right at work? What did he do wrong?

George left the restaurant. He felt
bad about eating the chef's food.

On the way home, he wondered if there
was a job for monkeys who like to eat.

Later, he found one . . .

"Finish everything on your plate, George."
George was the right monkey for the job.

A chef is a worker that makes food. Can you name other
workers that make or grow food?

215

George Sees...

What does George see on his way to work?
Write the missing vowel.

a e i o u

It's a d_g.

It's a j_t.

It's a c_t.

It's a b_s.

It's a k_d.

A Good Start

Say the name of each picture. Match pictures that make the same beginning sound.

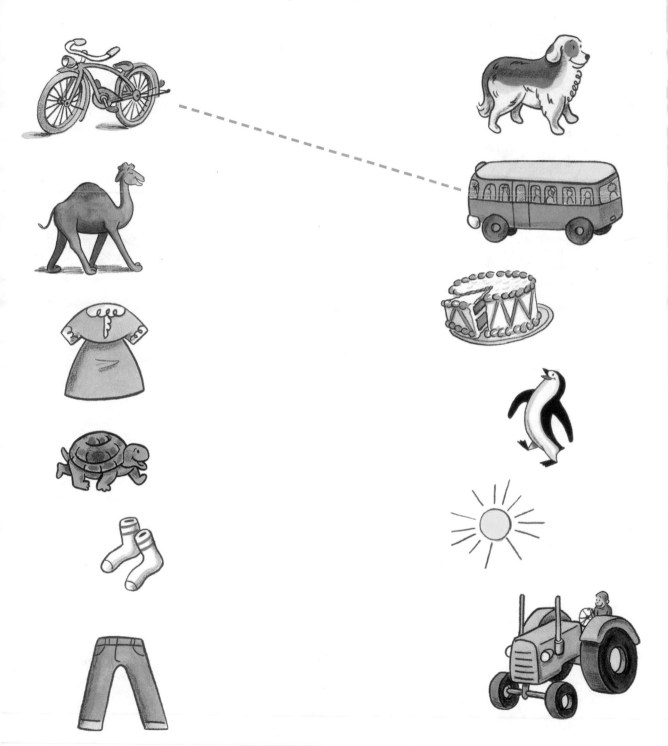

Who is driving the tractor? It is ____armer George!

217

A Good Ending

Say the name of each picture. Match pictures that make the same ending sound.

What did the chef make?
Write a letter to finish each dish.

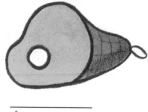

ha___   pizz___   sala___

Who Is Talking?

"It is time for recess!" said the teacher.
Circle the teacher.

Now who is talking? Read each sentence.
Circle who said it.

"I can catch it," said .

"I like to swing," said .

"I am almost at the top," said   .

"Hold on tight, George!" said   .

219

Stack Them

The chef wants George to stack ten dishes. Draw more to make ten. Then complete the number sentence.

$1 + \underline{} = 10$

$2 + \underline{} = 10$

$3 + \underline{} = 10$

$4 + \underline{} = 10$

Ten Dollars

George earns $10 at work. Circle two gifts in each row that add up to $10.

$7 $6 $4

$9 $4 $1

$3 $6 $7

Sweets for Sale

George sells sweets.

A customer wants $5 + 5 + 4$ cupcakes.

That's the same as ___10___ + 4 cupcakes.

So, $5 + 5 + 4 = 10 +$ ___4___

$3 + 7 + 6 = 10 +$ ____

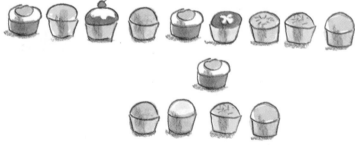

$9 + 1 + 4 = 10 +$ ____

$7 + 6 + 4 =$ ____ $+ 10$

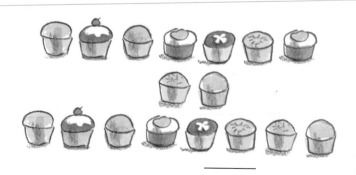

$7 + 2 + 8 =$ ____ $+ 10$

George stacks cupcakes.
Circle two numbers to add first. Write the sum
of the two numbers. Then find the total sum.

4
4
+ 6
___
14

7
3
+ 3
___

2
2
+ 8
___

4
3
+ 3
___

5
5
+ 4
___

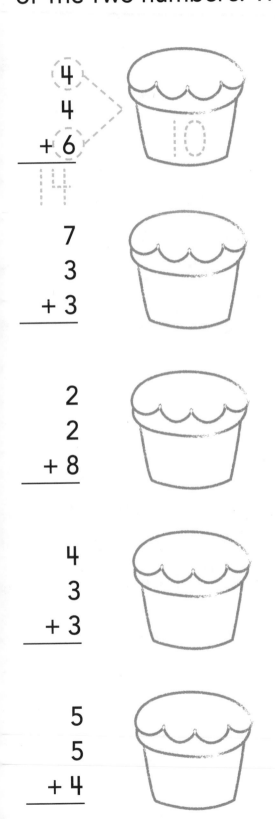

Water Works!

Water is a natural resource.
Trace to show how people use it at work and home.

⟂ puts out fires.

⟂ cleans dishes.

It is your job to protect water. One way is to turn off the faucets.

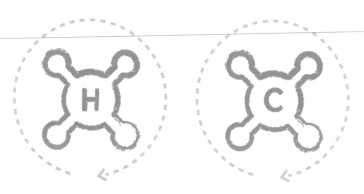

⟂ cleans George!

Made for You!

It is someone's job to make the things you wear, play with, and read. Circle things that are made with natural materials.

A ⟨natural⟩ material, like wool, is found in nature.

A ⟨human-made⟩ material, like plastic, is made in a lab.

cotton underwear

wool coat

nylon kite

plastic yo-yo

book

Good Job!

A chore is a small job. Do you help with these chores? Circle **yes** or **no**.

I make my bed.

yes　　**no**

I set the table.

yes　　**no**

I put my clothes away.

yes　　**no**

I feed my pet.

yes　　**no**

I don't have one!

My favorite chore is:

_____

_____

My least favorite chore is:

_____

_____

You did it!

Make an **X** next to things you know.

Place a sticker

☐ I can match words that make the same **beginning** or **ending** sounds.

☐ I know who is telling a story.

☐ I know different ways to **make 10**.

☐ I know a new way to add three numbers.

☐ I know that water is a **natural resource**. I use it every day.

☐ I know that workers make things using **natural** and **human-made** materials.

☐ I can do chores to help at home.

Happy Birthday

George is curious about . . .

 Reading   adjectives; writing dates; possessive nouns; high-frequency words

 Math   subtracting within 20; using symbols to compare

 Science   temperature: hot and cold; weight: heavy and light

 Social and Emotional   showing kindness

Happy Birthday, George!

George was having
a birthday party.
The man helped him
write the invitations.

He wrote on each one,
"Please come to my party."
Then George signed it.

George wanted all
of his friends to come
to the party.
He wondered how to
make the invitation
sound more exciting.

George had an idea. He added some words.
"Please come to my party *in space*."
George pictured his party in the stars.

But, oh! It was too hard
to eat cake in space.

Why might it be hard to eat cake in space? Imagine that you
have been invited to a party in space. How will you get there?

231

So George wrote instead,
"Please come to my party *in the clouds*."
What fun!

But, oh! Who would sing *Happy Birthday*
to George? The hot air balloon was too
small for his friends.

So George wrote instead,
"Please come to my party *in a castle*."
A castle was exciting.
And it was big enough for his friends,
his friends' friends, and his friends'
friends' friends!

But, oh! George did not live in a castle.
He lived in a house. So George simply
asked, "Please come to my party."

Would you prefer to have a party in a balloon or a castle? Why?
Where does George decide to have his party?

233

It was the day of the party.
George's friends arrived one by one.
The party was not in space, in the clouds,
or in a castle. Yet everybody came!

They sang. They played
games. George blew out
the candles.

"Happy Birthday, George!" said his friend.
"I would not have missed your party
for the world!"

A Fun Party

Describe the party. Write the best adjective to describe each noun.

green   **happy**   **red**   **soft**

George saw a _____ present.

It had a _____ bow.

George opened it.

It was a _____ teddy bear.

George was a _____ monkey!

Color in George's party hat.
Then describe it.

It's a _____ party hat.

Presents!

George opened his presents.
The children played with them.
Write an adjective to describe each one.

green   loud   round   striped   yellow

_____
_____ duck

_____
_____ ball

_____
_____ dinosaur

_____
_____ horn

_____
_____ puppet

A Special Day

George wants to remember special days.
Show him how to write each date correctly.

The boy had a birthday party on may 20 2014.

May 20, 2014

The dog had puppies on august 1 2014.

_____

. . . .

_____

The toy store opened on march 23 2012.

_____

. . . .

_____

Draw yourself and a friend.

This is me.   This is _____.

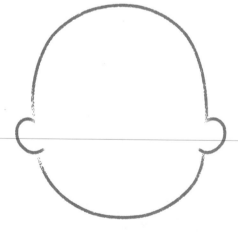 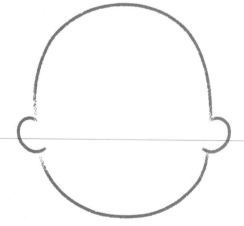

I was born on   (He / She) was born on

_____   _____

. . . .

_____ .   _____ .

George's Friend

A possessive noun tells who owns something.

It is ___George's___ friend!

Use the words to complete each sentence.

dog's

elephant's

frog's

girl's

tree's

The _____ shoes are blue.

The _____ tail is long.

The _____ legs are green.

The _____ trunk is brown.

But the _____ trunk is gray!

Birthday Cake

George makes a cake. Write the best word to complete each sentence.

George _____ eggs into a bowl.

      puts   cuts

He stirs the batter with his _____.

      face   feet

It is too much _____.

      work   play

So George turns the mixer _____.

      around   on

Oh no! _____ it is too fast!

    Then   Now

George tries to _____

make it _____ .

stop   go

The batter flies all _____ the room.

high   over

George gets an idea. He _____ the door.

opens   closes

Some puppies _____ in.

made   run

They _____ clean up the mess!

help   eat

A Friend's Party

George goes to a birthday party.

There are 14 children at the party. 11 go home.
How many children are still at the party?

$$14 - 11 = 3$$

_____ children

The boy has 12 presents. He opens 7.
How many are left to open?

_____ - _____ = _____

_____ presents

There are 18 balloons. *Oops!* George pops 5.
How many balloons are left?

_____ - _____ = _____

_____ balloons

Balloon Time!

Color in the balloon that makes the number sentence true.

15 − 3 2 = 12

11 − 2 3 = 8

12 − 5 6 = 6

16 − 8 6 = 10

17 − 4 6 = 13

Greater Than

Compare the number of candles on each cake.

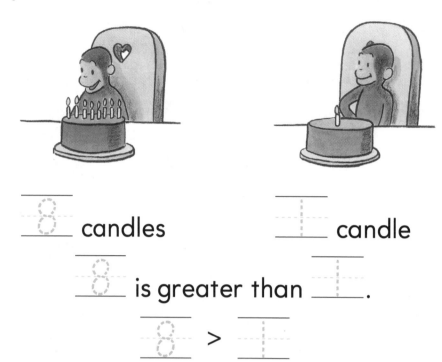

_8_ candles   _1_ candle

_8_ is greater than _1_.

_8_ > _1_

Write the numbers to compare.
The > points to the smaller number.

Compare 20 and 15.

_____ is greater than _____.   _____ > _____

Compare 35 and 31.

_____ is greater than _____.   _____ > _____

Compare 44 and 74.

_____ is greater than _____.   _____ > _____

Piñata Party!

The piñata burst!
The children pick up candies.

15 (<) 18

This symbol
means
is less than.

18 (=) 18

This symbol
means
is equal to.

23 (>) 18

This symbol
means
is greater than.

Compare the numbers.

21 (<) 29   21 __is less than__ 29

12 ( ) 12   12 _____ 12

34 ( ) 33   34 _____ 33

51 ( ) 57   51 _____ 57

75 ( ) 66   75 _____ 65

George picked up the most candies.
Find the **greatest** number above.

_____

George has _____ candies.

245

Birthday Treats

George eats hot and cold food
at the birthday party.

__Temperature__ is the measure
of how hot or cold something is.

Is it hot or cold? Circle one.

hot   cold

hot   cold

hot   cold

hot   cold

Draw one more treat for the party.
Is it hot or cold?

hot   cold

What's in the Box?

George picks up a box.
It is light. It is not heavy.

Weight is the measure
of how heavy an object feels.

Can you guess what's inside? Circle which is lighter.

A jar of candy   A rubber duck

Order these gifts from lightest to heaviest.
Write **1** for lightest. Write **3** for heaviest.

A is (**heavier** / **lighter**) than a .

How Kind!

George has kind friends.

The girl hugs George on his special day.

The boy helps George cross the street.

How kind!

Show how you can be kind to someone else. Check each box.

☐ I can say "thank you."

☐ I can help someone without being asked.

☐ I can draw a picture for someone.

☐ I can share my toys.

☐ I can ask someone how they feel. "How are you?"

You did it!

Make an **X** next to things you know.

Place a sticker

☐ I can describe how something **looks** or **feels**.

☐ I know how to write my birthday.

☐ I can add **'s** to tell who owns something. It is George's birthday!

☐ I know the words **face**, **feet**, **play**, and **work** on sight.

☐ I can **subtract** to solve a **word problem**.

☐ I know that 10 is **greater than** 5, and 5 is **less than** 10.

☐ I can use symbols to compare numbers.

☐ I know that the **temperature** is the measure of **how hot or cold** something is.

☐ I know that **weight** is the measure of **how heavy** something feels.

☐ I am kind to others.

Turn the page to start a new adventure!

Farm to Table

George is curious about . . .

Reading   high-frequency words; past, present, and future verbs

Math   tally charts;
shape attributes;
equal parts;
halves and fourths

Science   plant parts;
plants and animals

Social and Emotional   table manners

Farm to Monkey

George and
the man were going
food shopping.
George loved to visit
the supermarket.

It had long aisles to run down.
It had high shelves to climb.

But this was not the
right way. George
pointed. The supermarket
was the other way.

"The farmers market is open today," said the man.

A farm was a fun place to visit. George could pick apples right off a tree! But this was not the way to the farm.

An apple farm is called an orchard. What can you make with apples? Have you ever picked a peck of apples? A peck is about 35 apples.

George and the man turned the
corner. At the end of the street
was an outdoor market.

"Good morning," said the
man in the white apron. He
sold fruits and vegetables.
But he also grew them.
He was a farmer.

One day a week, he loaded ripe fruits
and vegetables onto a truck.
He drove them into town to sell them.

The farmer visits town one day a week. What do you think
he does on other days? The farmer brings ripe fruits
and vegetables to town. What does *ripe* mean?

George saw yellow corn
and crunchy carrots.
He smelled sweet oranges.
He plucked an orange
out of the pile.
They all tumbled down.

"Oh no," said the farmer.
"The oranges are bruised.
Now I cannot sell them."
George frowned.

"Don't worry," said the
man with the yellow hat.
"We'll buy them all."
George wondered how
they could eat so many.

At home, they squeezed the oranges to make orange juice. It tasted extra sweet and delicious.

George couldn't wait to visit the farmer's market next week.

 A farmer's market is different than a supermarket because you can meet the people who grow the food. What would you ask a farmer about the food he or she grows?

Apples!

George visited a farm. Write the correct word to complete each sentence.

George _____ to the apple farm.

went   gone

He spent the day _____.

inside   outside

He climbed to the _____ of a tree.

top   behind

He _____ an apple to the farmer.

gave   have

"Thank you, George," _____ said.

her   she

George saw something _____ the tree.

across   behind

It was a _____ made out of hay.

man   father

"_____ is a scarecrow," said the farmer.

That   My

"It _____ the animals from eating my apples."

finds   stops

_____ it did not stop George!

But   Then

Yesterday!

Tell what happened yesterday.
Circle the correct verb.
Then write the sentence.

George (**plays / played**) in the hay.

_____

George (**picks / picked**) apples.

_____

George (**collects / collected**) eggs.

_____

The chicks (**chirp / chirped**).

_____

Tomorrow!

Circle the sentences that tell what the farmer will do in the future.

The farmer will feed the animals.

The farmer plants seeds.

The farmer will pick apples.

The farmer milks the cows.

The farmer will sell the apples.

Draw a line under sentences you did not circle. Rewrite them to tell about the future.

The farmer will _____

_____

_____ .

_____

_____

_____ .

261

On the Farm

George counts the red and green
apple trees at the farm.

	Apple Trees	Total
🍎 trees	||||	4
🍏 trees	|||| ||	7

(Color it in.)
There are more 🍎 apple trees.

The farmer plants the trees in a pattern.
Complete the pattern in each row.

How many chickens, cows, and sheep
are on the farm? Make a tally chart.
Cross out each animal as you count it.

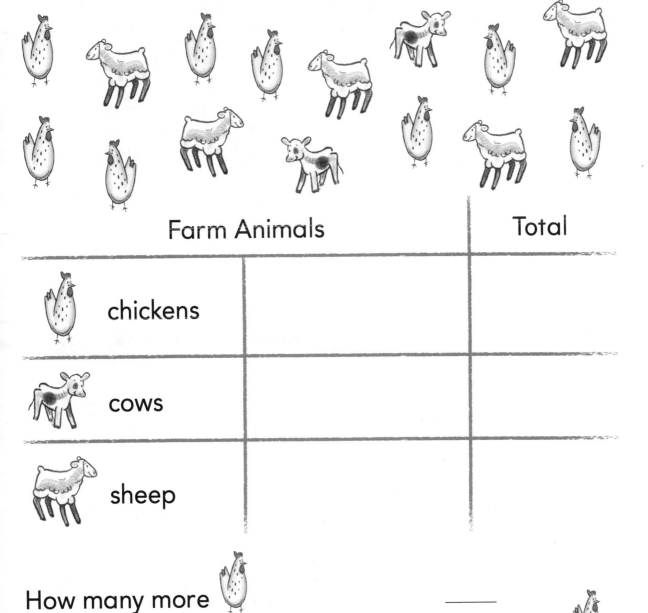

Farm Animals		Total
chickens		
cows		
sheep		

How many more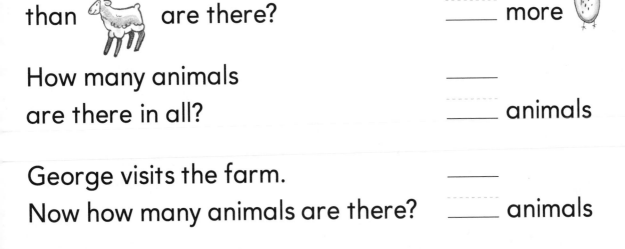
than are there?   _____ more

How many animals
are there in all?   _____ animals

George visits the farm.   _____
Now how many animals are there?   _____ animals

263

Chicken Coop

George sees many shapes at the farm.
Color in the shape you see on the coop.

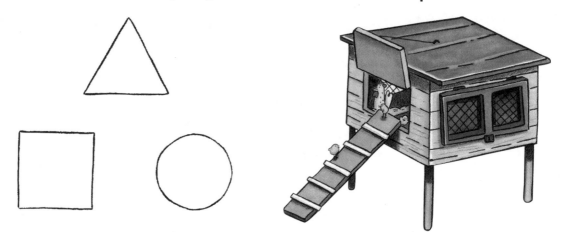

George holds a shape. Color it in.

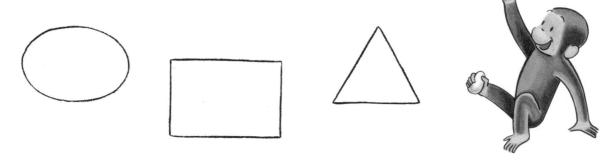

Color in shapes that are both curved and closed.

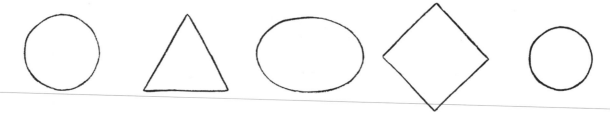

Color in shapes with 4 sides.

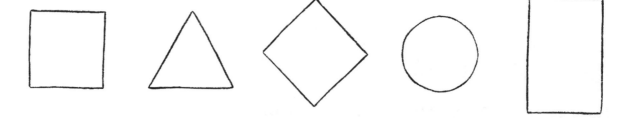

Time to Plant!

The farmer wants to grow carrots. Plow the soil.
Color in shapes that show **equal parts**.

 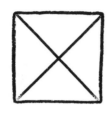 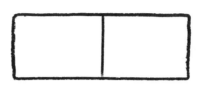 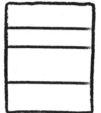

This shape shows 2 equal parts, or **halves**.
The farmer plants carrot seeds in 1 half.

c c c c c	
c c c c c	
c c c c c	

Plant carrot seeds in the other half.

The farmer wants to plant more crops.
Draw lines to show 4 equal parts, or **fourths**.

Plant beans in 1 fourth. Plant lettuce in 1 fourth.
Plant peppers in 1 fourth. Plant your favorite
fruit or vegetable in the last fourth.

My favorite vegetable is _____.

Growing Up

George needs room to grow. So do plants!
As a plant grows, its roots get bigger.
It grows more leaves.

Draw an adult plant.

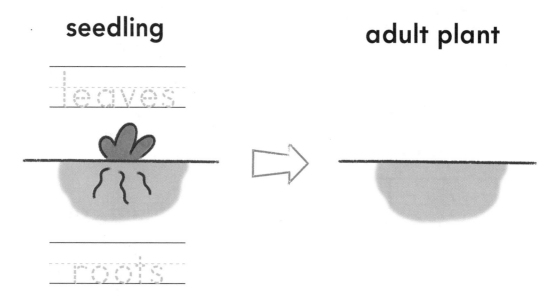

seedling   **adult plant**

leaves

roots

Use the words to complete each plant fact.

stem   **roots**   **water**

The _____ grow into the soil.

They take in _____
that the plant needs.

A _____ carries water to other plant parts.

Use the words to complete each plant fact.

flower   **fruits**   **leaf**   **seed**

A _____ is a plant part that makes food for the plant.

A _____ makes seeds.

A new plant may grow from a _____.

Many flowers grow into _____ that hold seeds.

Circle the part that makes food for the plant.
Make an **X** on the part that holds seeds.

267

Plant Parts

Farm to Tummy

People and animals use plants for food.

The orange tree makes _flowers_.

Some flowers grow into _fruits_.

Then George eats them!

What else goes from the farm to *your* tummy?
Draw two things.

268

Life at the Farm

Plants and animals live at the farm.
Show how they are the same or different.
Write **yes** or **no** to complete the chart.

makes its own food	yes	
eats plants or animals		
moves around on its own		
grows and changes		

A green plant uses **air**, **water**, and **light**
to make food. Label each picture.

_____

_____

Farm to Table Manners

Tell George how to use
good table manners.
Circle the words.

(**Stand / Sit**) at the table.

Wash your hands (**before / after**) eating.

Take (**big / small**) bites.

(**Do not / Do**) play at the table.

Chew with your mouth (**closed / open**).

Eat with your (**fork / hands**).

What's for dinner? Set a place for George.
Then draw food on the plate.

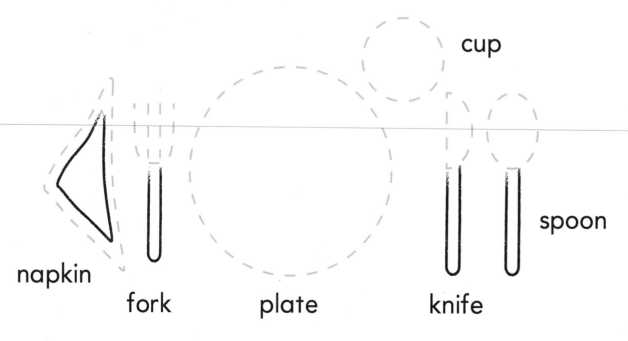

cup

napkin

fork   plate   knife

spoon

You did it!

Make an **X** next to things you know.

Place a sticker

☐ I know the words **went**, **outside**, and **top** on sight.

☐ I can choose the correct words to tell what happened **yesterday** and what will happen in the **future**.

☐ I can make a **tally chart** to show how many.

☐ I know that a **square** and a **rectangle** have four sides. A **circle** and **oval** are curved.

☐ I can cut a shape into **halves** and **fourths**.

☐ I know that plants **grow and change**.

☐ I know the names of plant parts: **seed**, **leaf**, **flower**, and **fruit**.

☐ I know that a plant makes food in its leaf.

☐ I use **good table manners**.

You did it!

Play Together

Phonics Cards

Fold and glue.

Fold and glue.

Cut out and fold!

b

ball

d

dog

f

fish

g

girl

h

hat

j

jar

k

kite

l

leaf

m

monkey

n

nest

ng

sing

p

pizza

r

rainbow

s

sun

Search for Sounds

Phonics cards

1. Ask your child to pick a card.

2. Say the name of the picture. Emphasize the *underlined* sound. *Ex.* ball

3. Ask your child to find something at home that has the same sound. A *banana*, a *baby*, a *bathtub*. How many can she find?

Play on the go! Search outside, in a park, or at a restaurant!

 Cut out and play!

275

g	**f**	**d**	**b**
e<u>gg</u>	<u>f</u>an	<u>d</u>rum	<u>b</u>at
<u>g</u>et	<u>f</u>ork	han<u>d</u>	<u>b</u>ike
<u>g</u>o	<u>ph</u>one	sala<u>d</u>	ra<u>bb</u>it

l	**k**	**j**	**h**
be<u>ll</u>	ba<u>k</u>e	<u>c</u>age	<u>h</u>en
<u>l</u>eg	<u>k</u>id	<u>j</u>elly	<u>h</u>ot
<u>l</u>ook	la<u>k</u>e	<u>j</u>ump	<u>wh</u>o

p	**ng**	**n**	**m**
a<u>pp</u>le	kin<u>g</u>	di<u>nn</u>er	ha<u>mm</u>er
<u>p</u>ie	rin<u>g</u>	<u>kn</u>ee	la<u>mb</u>
<u>p</u>ig	swin<u>g</u>	<u>n</u>o	<u>m</u>ouse

This or That?
Phonics cards

1. Hold up 2 cards so that your child can see the pictures.
2. A word list is on the back of each card. Read one word from either list. Emphasize the *underlined* sound. *Ex.* ra<u>bb</u>it
3. Ask your child to point to the pictured word that has the same sound.

Extend it! Ask your child to think of a new word that has the same sound.

s	**r**
<u>c</u>ity	<u>c</u>arrot
dre<u>ss</u>	<u>r</u>obot
i<u>c</u>e	<u>wr</u>ite

t	**v**	**w**	**y**

<u>t</u>eddy	<u>v</u>alentine	<u>w</u>agon	<u>y</u>o-yo

z	**zh**	**ch**	**sh**

<u>z</u>ebra	trea<u>s</u>ure	<u>ch</u>ips	<u>sh</u>eep

soft th	**hard th**	**short a**	**short e**

<u>th</u>ank	fea<u>th</u>er	<u>a</u>pple	<u>e</u>lephant

short i	**short o**	**short u**	**short oo**

<u>i</u>gloo	<u>o</u>strich	<u>u</u>mbrella	b<u>oo</u>k

 Cut out and play!

y	**w**	**v**	**t**
on<u>i</u>on	<u>o</u>ne	gi<u>v</u>e	ca<u>t</u>
<u>y</u>ellow	<u>w</u>et	o<u>f</u>	le<u>tt</u>er
<u>y</u>es	<u>w</u>ind	<u>v</u>an	<u>t</u>op

sh	**ch**	**zh**	**z**
<u>sh</u>e	bea<u>ch</u>	gara<u>g</u>e	bu<u>zz</u>
<u>sh</u>oe	lun<u>ch</u>	mea<u>s</u>ure	i<u>s</u>
<u>sh</u>op	wa<u>tch</u>	televi<u>si</u>on	<u>z</u>ip

short e	**short a**	**hard th**	**soft th**
b<u>e</u>d	<u>a</u>nt	mo<u>th</u>er	ba<u>th</u>
br<u>ea</u>d	b<u>a</u>t	<u>th</u>e	<u>th</u>umb
<u>e</u>gg	p<u>a</u>rrot	wi<u>th</u>	too<u>th</u>

short oo	**short u**	**short o**	**short i**
c<u>oo</u>k	b<u>u</u>g	d<u>o</u>ll	g<u>y</u>m
p<u>u</u>ll	n<u>u</u>t	fr<u>o</u>g	k<u>i</u>tten
w<u>oo</u>l	s<u>o</u>n	h<u>o</u>t	m<u>i</u>lk

long a	**long e**	**long i**	**long o**

c<u>a</u>ke	tr<u>ee</u>	p<u>ie</u>	c<u>oa</u>t

long u	**long oo**	**oi**	**ow**

<u>u</u>niform	m<u>oo</u>n	c<u>oi</u>n	c<u>ow</u>

air	**ar**	**ir**	**aw**

ch<u>air</u>	c<u>ar</u>	b<u>ir</u>d	p<u>aw</u>

ear	**ure**	**x**	**qu**
		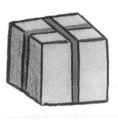	
<u>ear</u>	pict<u>ure</u>	bo<u>x</u>	<u>qu</u>ilt

 Cut out and play!

long o	long i	long e	long a
b**o**n**e**	b**i**k**e**	f**ee**t	**a**p**e**
oval	f**i**ve	k**e**y	pl**a**y
s**oa**p	l**i**on	s**ee**	r**ai**n

ow	oi	long oo	long u
fr**ow**n	b**oy**	p**oo**l	c**u**t**e**
me**ow**	j**oy**	r**u**ler	gl**ue**
sh**ou**t	s**oi**l	sp**oo**n	j**ui**ce

aw	ir	ar	air
cl**aw**	f**ir**st	f**ar**	b**ear**
dr**aw**	t**ur**n	j**ar**	h**air**
y**aw**n	w**or**k	st**ar**	sq**uare**

qu	x	ure	ear
queen	e**x**it	inj**ure**	ch**eer**
quick	fo**x**	nat**ure**	h**ear**
quiet	so**c**ks	s**ure**	st**eer**

Number Cards

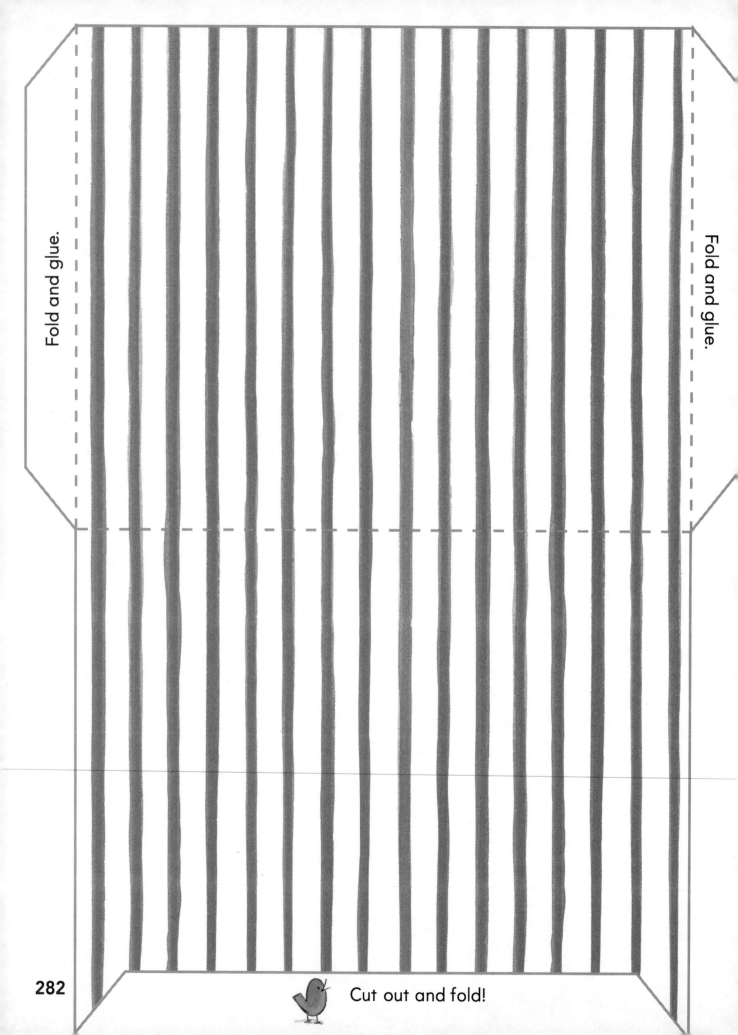

Fold and glue.

Fold and glue.

Cut out and fold!

1	2	3	4	5	6	7	8	9	10
11	12	13	14	15	16	17	18	19	20
21	22	23	24	25	26	27	28	29	30
31	32	33	34	35	36	37	38	39	40
41	42	43	44	45	46	47	48	49	50
51	52	53	54	55	56	57	58	59	60
61	62	63	64	65	66	67	68	69	70
71	72	73	74	75	76	77	78	79	80
81	82	83	84	85	86	87	88	89	90
91	92	93	94	95	96	97	98	99	100
101	102	103	104	105	106	107	108	109	110
111	112	113	114	115	116	117	118	119	120

Penny Drop

Number chart, 1 penny

1. Drop a penny onto the chart.

2. Count up by 1s from where the penny landed.

3. Or skip count from where the penny landed:

- by 2s: ...30, 32, 34, 36, 38...
- by 5s: ...30, 35, 40, 45, 50...
- by 10s: ...30, 40, 50, 60, 70...

1	2	3	4	5	6	7		9	10
11	12	13	14		16	17	18	19	20
21	22	23	24	25	26		28	29	30
31		33	34	35	36	37	38	39	40
41	42	43	44	45		47	48	49	50
51	52	53	54	55	56	57	58		60
61	62		64	65	66	67	68	69	70
71	72	73		75	76	77	78	79	80
	82	83	84	85	86	87	88	89	90
91	92	93	94	95	96	97	98	99	
101	102	103	104		106	107	108	109	110
111	112	113	114	115	116		118	119	120

Stack 'Em!

Number chart, pennies

1. Ask your child to close her eyes.

2. Use pennies to cover up any 3 numbers in the same row. *Ex.* 1, _, 3, 4, _, 6, 7, 8, _, 10

3. Now ask your child to count up from the beginning of the row.
   Can she name the hidden numbers? Stack 1 penny for each number.

4. Play for ten minutes. How many pennies did she stack?

Complete the chart. Write in the missing numbers!

0   1   2   3

4   5   6   7

8   9   10

Ice Cream Cone

Number cards 0–10

1. Place 3 cards faceup.

2. Find the sum of each pair from top to bottom.

3. Find the final sum!

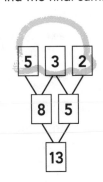

 Cut out and play!

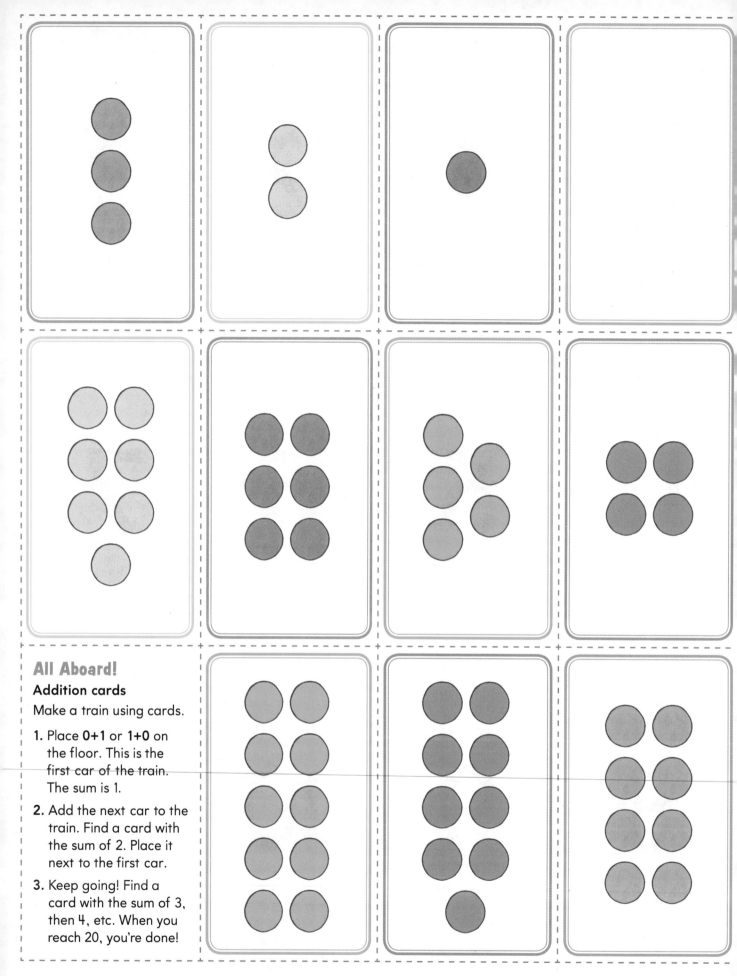

All Aboard!
Addition cards
Make a train using cards.

1. Place **0+1** or **1+0** on the floor. This is the first car of the train. The sum is 1.

2. Add the next car to the train. Find a card with the sum of 2. Place it next to the first car.

3. Keep going! Find a card with the sum of 3, then 4, etc. When you reach 20, you're done!

0 1 2 3

4 5 6 7

8 9 10

Top Banana
Addition cards
1. Deal 18 cards to each player.
2. Each player turns over 1 card to show the addition side. The player with the higher sum keeps both cards.
   Ex. 8+6 beats 9+2
3. If the sums are the same, each player must turn over a new card. The player with the higher total keeps all four cards.

 Cut out and play!

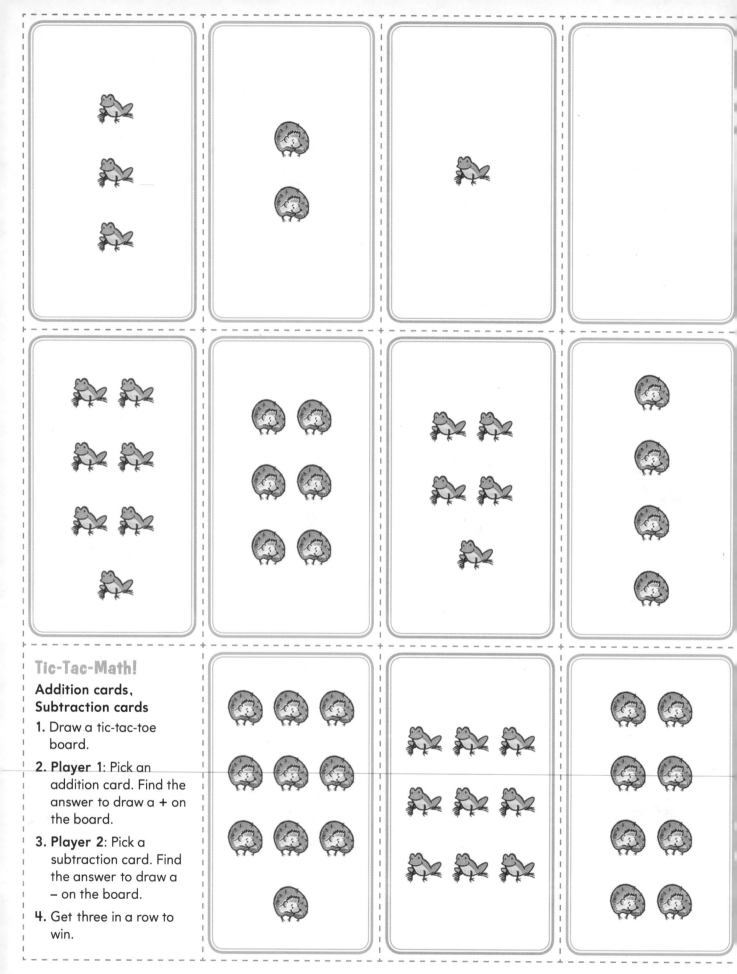

Tic-Tac-Math!

Addition cards, Subtraction cards

1. Draw a tic-tac-toe board.

2. **Player 1**: Pick an addition card. Find the answer to draw a + on the board.

3. **Player 2**: Pick a subtraction card. Find the answer to draw a – on the board.

4. Get three in a row to win.

11 12 13 14

15 16 17 18

19 20

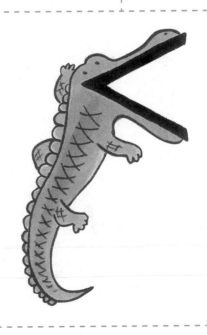

Cut out and play!

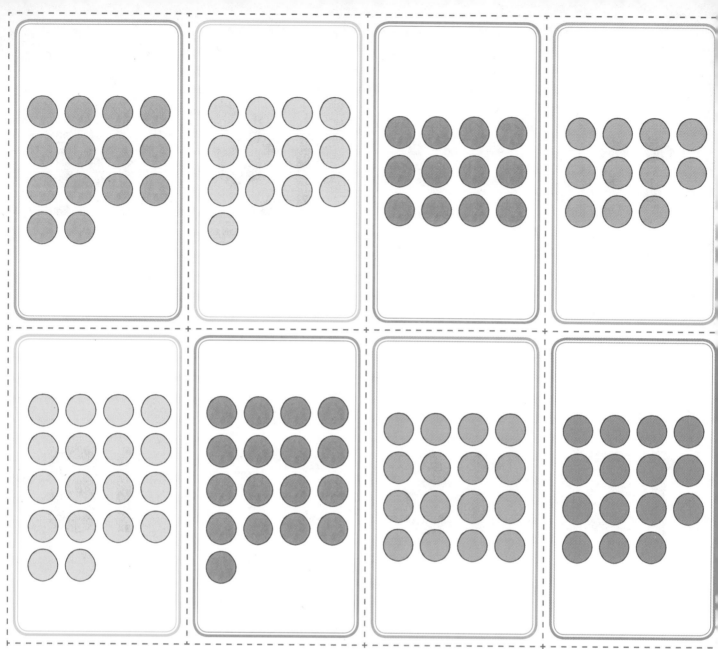

Chomp!

Number cards, Alligator cards (< and >)

1. Ask your child to pick 2 number cards. Lay them faceup with a space in between. *Ex.* 7_6

2. Tell him that the **<** and **>** symbols are like an alligator's mouth. It is hungry and wants to eat the greater number.

3. Ask your child to place an alligator in between the numbers. It must show the alligator eating the greater number.

4. Read the final sentence. *Ex.* If **7 > 6**, then say "7 is *greater than* 6. The alligator ate the 7." *Ex.* If **6 < 7**, then say "6 is *less than* 7. The alligator ate the 7."

5. Play for 10 minutes. How many cards did the alligator eat?

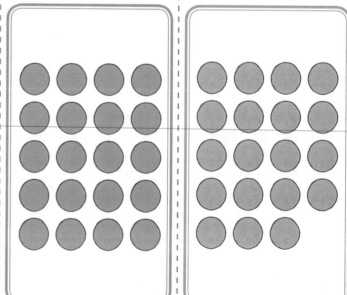

11 12 13 14

15 16 17 18

19 20

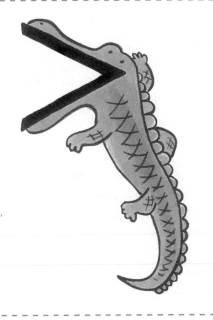

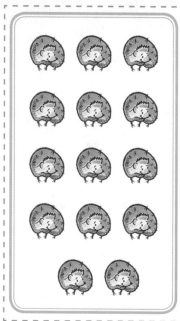 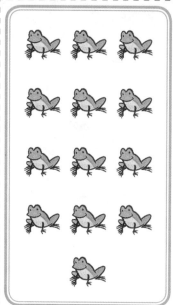 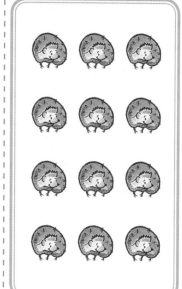 

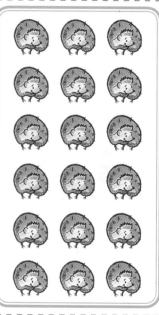  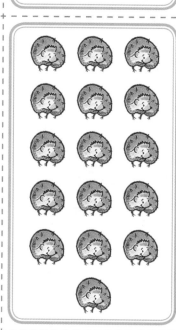 

Number Fish!

Addition or Subtraction cards

1. Make 20 same-answer pairs. *Ex.* **1+6** and **3+4**. Shuffle them. Deal 5 cards to each player. Put the remaining cards in a facedown pile.

2. Check your cards. Do you have 2 cards with the same sum? It's a pair! Put it aside.

3. **Player** 1: Try to make a pair. For example, if you hold **2+3**, you may ask Player 2, "Do you have a 5?"
Player 2: If you hold a card with this sum (ex. **4+1**), hand it over. If not, tell Player 1, "Fish for it!" Player 1 takes a card from the pile.

4. **Player** 2: It's your turn! Ask Player 1 for a sum.

5. Keep going until one player has no more cards. Who made the most pairs?

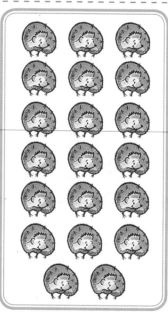 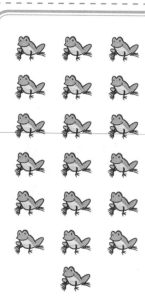

$0 + 1$	$1 + 0$	$1 + 1$
$1 + 2$	$1 + 3$	$2 + 2$
$1 + 4$	$2 + 3$	$1 + 5$
$2 + 4$	$3 + 3$	$1 + 6$
$2 + 5$	$3 + 4$	$1 + 7$

 Cut out and play!

19 – 0	2 – 1	5 – 4
9 – 8	11 – 10	14 – 13
18 – 17	20 – 19	3 – 1
5 – 3	7 – 5	11 – 9
12 – 10	14 – 12	16 – 14

2 + 6	3 + 5	4 + 4
1 + 8	2 + 7	3 + 6
4 + 5	10 + 0	1 + 9
2 + 8	3 + 7	4 + 6
5 + 5	1 + 10	2 + 9

 Cut out and play!

18 – 16	4 – 1	6 – 3
8 – 5	10 – 7	12 – 9
13 – 10	15 – 12	17 – 14
19 – 16	5 – 1	7 – 3
9 – 5	11 – 7	13 – 9

3 + 8	4 + 7	5 + 6
1 + 11	2 + 10	3 + 9
4 + 8	5 + 7	6 + 6
1 + 12	2 + 11	3 + 10
4 + 9	5 + 8	6 + 7

 Cut out and play!

14 – 10	16 – 12	18 – 14
20 – 16	7 – 2	9 – 4
11 – 6	13 – 8	14 – 9
16 – 11	18 – 13	20 – 15
8 – 2	10 – 4	12 – 6

$1 + 13$	$2 + 12$	$3 + 11$
$4 + 10$	$5 + 9$	$6 + 8$
$7 + 7$	$0 + 2$	$1 + 14$
$2 + 13$	$3 + 12$	$4 + 11$
$5 + 10$	$6 + 9$	$7 + 8$

Cut out and play!

14 – 8	15 – 9	17 – 11
19 – 13	9 – 2	11 – 4
13 – 6	14 – 7	16 – 9
18 – 11	20 – 13	9 – 1
11 – 3	13 – 5	14 – 6

1 + 15	2 + 14	3 + 13
4 + 12	5 + 11	6 + 10
7 + 9	8 + 8	1 + 16
2 + 15	3 + 14	4 + 13
5 + 12	6 + 11	7 + 10

Cut out and play!

16 – 8	18 – 10	20 – 12
10 – 1	12 – 3	13 – 4
14 – 5	16 – 7	18 – 9
20 – 11	10 – 0	12 – 2
14 – 4	16 – 6	17 – 7

8 + 9	1 + 17	2 + 16
3 + 15	4 + 14	5 + 13
6 + 12	7 + 11	8 + 10
9 + 9	1 + 18	2 + 17
3 + 16	4 + 15	5 + 14

 Cut out and play!

13 – 2	15 – 4	17 – 6
19 – 8	13 – 1	15 – 3
17 – 5	18 – 6	20 – 8
14 – 1	16 – 3	18 – 5
20 – 7	15 – 1	17 – 3

6 + 13	7 + 12	8 + 11
9 + 10	3 + 0	1 + 19
2 + 18	3 + 17	4 + 16
5 + 15	6 + 14	7 + 13
8 + 12	9 + 11	10 + 10

Cut out and play!

19 − 5	15 − 0	16 − 1
17 − 2	18 − 3	20 − 5
17 − 1	18 − 2	20 − 4
18 − 1	19 − 2	19 − 1
20 − 2	20 − 1	20 − 0

Answers

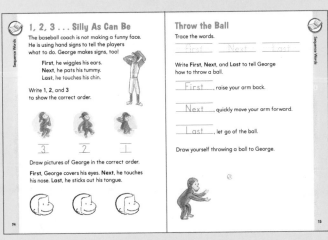

1, 2, 3 . . . Silly As Can Be

The baseball coach is not making a funny face. He is using hand signs to tell the players what to do. George makes signs, too!

First, he wiggles his ears.
Next, he pats his tummy.
Last, he touches his chin.

Write **1**, **2**, and **3** to show the correct order.

3   2   1

Draw pictures of George in the correct order.

First, George covers his eyes. **Next**, he touches his nose. **Last**, he sticks out his tongue.

Throw the Ball

Trace the words.

First   Next   Last

Write **First**, **Next**, and **Last** to tell George how to throw a ball.

First , raise your arm back.

Next , quickly move your arm forward.

Last , let go of the ball.

Draw yourself throwing a ball to George.

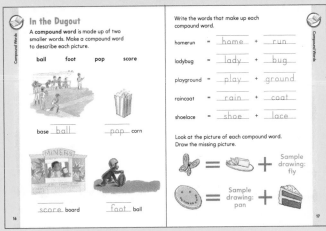

In the Dugout

A **compound word** is made up of two smaller words. Make a compound word to describe each picture.

ball   foot   pop   score

base ball   pop corn

score board   foot ball

Write the words that make up each compound word.

homerun	=	home	+	run
ladybug	=	lady	+	bug
playground	=	play	+	ground
raincoat	=	rain	+	coat
shoelace	=	shoe	+	lace

Look at the picture of each compound word. Draw the missing picture.

= Sample drawing: fly +

= + Sample drawing: pan

Play Ball!

Tell what is happening at the game. Choose a word to complete each sentence.

ball   batter   cheer   pitcher   team

The pitcher throws the ball.

The batter swings the bat.

The ball flies far.

The fans cheer .

Their team is winning!

The camera is pointed at you! Draw yourself cheering.

Fly Ball!

Write the missing word in each sentence.

and   people   first   time   He

The batter swings and misses.

He swings again.

This time , he hits the ball.

He runs to first base.

The people cheer.

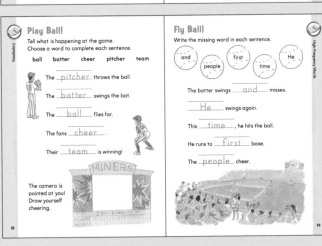

Connect the Shapes

Draw a line from each flat shape to a solid shape. Then draw a line from the solid shape to an object.

circle   cube
rectangle   sphere
square   rectangular prism

One ball is not a sphere. Make an X on it.

How Tall?

George is about 5 baseballs tall. About how tall is each friend?

Write a number.

about 14   about 10   about 5

One friend is about 5 baseballs taller than George. Circle him above.

How tall are you?   ____

I am about ____ tall.

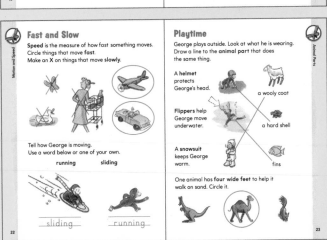

Fast and Slow

Speed is the measure of how fast something moves. Circle things that move **fast**. Make an X on things that move **slowly**.

Tell how George is moving. Use a word below or one of your own.

running   sliding

sliding   running

Playtime

George plays outside. Look at what he is wearing. Draw a line to the **animal part** that does the same thing.

A **helmet** protects George's head.   — a wooly coat

Flippers help George move underwater.   — a hard shell

A **snowsuit** keeps George warm.   — fins

One animal has **four wide feet** to help it walk on sand. Circle it.

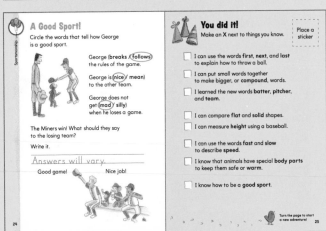

A Good Sport!

Circle the words that tell how George is a good sport.

George (breaks / follows) the rules of the game.

George is (nice / mean) to the other team.

George does not get (mad / silly) when he loses a game.

The Miners win! What should they say to the losing team?

Write it.

Answers will vary.

Good game!   Nice job!

You did it!

Make an X next to things you know.

Place a sticker

☐ I can use the words **first**, **next**, and **last** to explain how to throw a ball.

☐ I can put small words together to make bigger, or **compound**, words.

☐ I learned the new words **batter**, **pitcher**, and **team**.

☐ I can compare **flat** and **solid** shapes.

☐ I can measure **height** using a baseball.

☐ I can use the words **fast** and **slow** to describe **speed**.

☐ I know that animals have special **body parts** to keep them safe or warm.

☐ I know how to be a **good sport**.

Turn the page to start a new adventure!

Meow! Woof!

Compare the animals. Read each sentence.
Check the box if it describes the animal.
Then circle if they are **alike** or **different**.

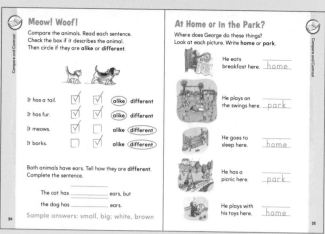

	🐱	🐶	
It has a tail.	☑	☑	(alike) different
It has fur.	☑	☑	(alike) different
It meows.	☑	☐	alike (different)
It barks.	☐	☑	alike (different)

Both animals have ears. Tell how they are **different**.
Complete the sentence.

The cat has _____ ears, but

the dog has _____ ears.

Sample answers: small, big; white, brown

At Home or in the Park?

Where does George do these things?
Look at each picture. Write **home** or **park**.

He eats
breakfast here. ___home___

He plays on
the swings here. ___park___

He goes to
sleep here. ___home___

He has a
picnic here. ___park___

He plays with
his toys here. ___home___

Shadow the Cat

Shadow starts with the **sh** sound.
Say the name of each picture.
Circle pictures that start with the **sh** sound.

Shadow

Did you get three in a row? Draw a line.

A Good Shelter

A shelter takes care of animals.
There are shelters for all kinds of animals.
Write **sh** or **ch** to finish the animal names.

___sheep___   ___fish___

___chick___   ___ostrich___

Who Am I?

Draw a line from the clue to the picture.

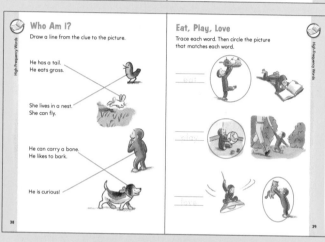

He has a tail.
He eats grass.

She lives in a nest.
She can fly.

He can carry a bone.
He likes to bark.

He is curious!

Eat, Play, Love

Trace each word. Then circle the picture
that matches each word.

___eat___

___play___

___love___

George's Scrapbook

George made a scrapbook.
Choose a word to write under each picture.

kitten   search   shelter   walk

___walk___

___search___

___shelter___   ___kitten___

Cats and Dogs

Are there more cats or dogs? Find out.
Color a square for each cat.
Color a square for each dog.

cat							
dog							

0 1 2 3 4 5 6 7

There are __2__ more cats than dogs.

Count the Animals

George counts 12 balls at the shelter.

12 = __1__ ten __2__ ones

Now count the animals.
Write the number in tens and ones.

__1__ ten __5__ ones

__1__ ten __8__ ones

__2__ tens __0__ ones

Animal Treats

Each box has 10 treats.
Write the number of treats in tens and ones.

__1__ tens __0__ ones
__10__ treats

__1__ ten __7__ ones
__17__ treats

__4__ tens __5__ ones
__45__ treats

__2__ tens __0__ ones
__20__ treats

Who Takes Care of Us?

Animal parents take care of their babies.
Draw a line from each sentence to a picture.

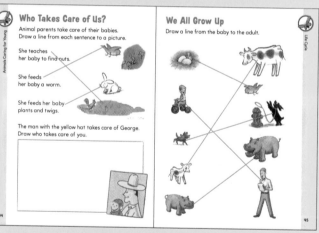

She teaches
her baby to find nuts.

She feeds
her baby a worm.

She feeds her baby
plants and twigs.

The man with the yellow hat takes care of George.
Draw who takes care of you.

We All Grow Up

Draw a line from the baby to the adult.

What Does It Need?

Do you want to take care of an animal?
Circle one.

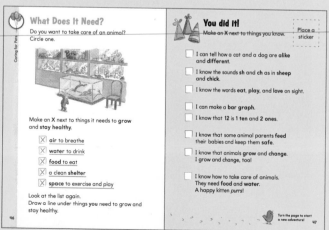

Make an X next to things it needs to **grow**
and **stay healthy**.

☒ **air** to breathe
☒ **water** to drink
☒ **food** to eat
☒ a clean **shelter**
☒ **space** to exercise and play

Look at the list again.
Draw a line under things **you** need to grow and
stay healthy.

You did it!

Make an X next to things you know.

Place a sticker

☐ I can tell how a cat and a dog are **alike**
and **different**.

☐ I know the sounds **sh** and **ch** as in **sheep**
and **chick**.

☐ I know the words **eat, play,** and **love** on sight.

☐ I can make a **bar graph**.

☐ I know that **12** is **1 ten** and **2 ones**.

☐ I know that some animal parents **feed**
their babies and keep them **safe**.

☐ I know that animals **grow** and **change**.
I grow and change, too!

☐ I know how to take care of animals.
They need **food** and **water**.
A happy kitten *purrs*!

Turn the page to start
a new adventure!

George Dreams

George dreams about his day at the factory.
Underline the sentences that describe
what he saw.

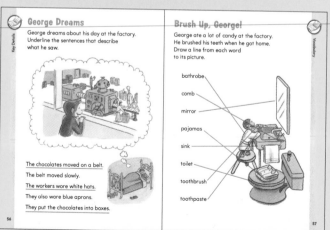

The chocolates moved on a belt.
The belt moved slowly.
The workers wore white hats.
They also wore blue aprons.
They put the chocolates into boxes.

Brush Up, George!

George ate a lot of candy at the factory.
He brushed his teeth when he got home.
Draw a line from each word
to its picture.

bathrobe
comb
mirror
pajamas
sink
toilet
toothbrush
toothpaste

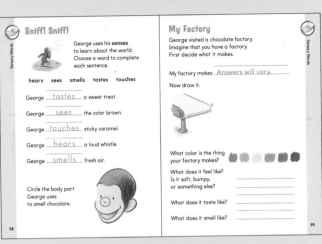

Sniff! Sniff!

George uses his **senses** to learn about the world. Choose a word to complete each sentence.

hears   sees   smells   tastes   touches

George _tastes_ a sweet treat.

George _sees_ the color brown.

George _touches_ sticky caramel.

George _hears_ a loud whistle.

George _smells_ fresh air.

Circle the body part George uses to smell chocolate.

58

My Factory

George visited a chocolate factory. Imagine that you have a factory. First decide what it makes.

My factory makes _Answers will vary._

Now draw it.

What color is the thing your factory makes?

What does it feel like? Is it soft, bumpy, or something else? _____

What does it taste like? _____

What does it smell like? _____

59

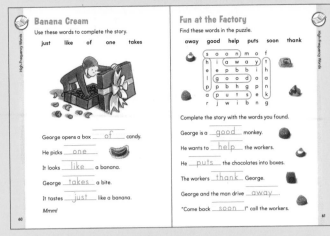

Banana Cream

Use these words to complete the story.

just   like   of   one   takes

George opens a box _of_ candy.

He picks _one_.

It looks _like_ a banana.

George _takes_ a bite.

It tastes _just_ like a banana.

Mmm!

60

Fun at the Factory

Find these words in the puzzle.

away   good   help   puts   soon   thank

```
s o o n m o f
h i a w a y e
e e p b i h l
p p b h g o p
a p u t s e e
r j w i b n g
```

Complete the story with the words you found.

George is a _good_ monkey.

He wants to _help_ the workers.

He _puts_ the chocolates into boxes.

The workers _thank_ George.

George and the man drive _away_.

"Come back _soon_!" call the workers.

61

This or That?

Read each question. Then write the answer.

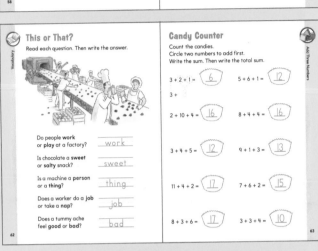

Do people **work** or **play** at a factory? _work_

Is chocolate a **sweet** or **salty** snack? _sweet_

Is a machine a **person** or a **thing**? _thing_

Does a worker do a **job** or take a **nap**? _job_

Does a tummy ache feel **good** or **bad**? _bad_

62

Candy Counter

Count the candies. Circle two numbers to add first. Write the sum. Then write the total sum.

$3 + 2 + 1 = 6$
$5 + 6 + 1 = 12$

$3 +$

$2 + 10 + 4 = 16$
$8 + 4 + 4 = 16$

$3 + 4 + 5 = 12$
$9 + 1 + 3 = 13$

$11 + 4 + 2 = 17$
$7 + 6 + 2 = 15$

$8 + 3 + 6 = 17$
$3 + 3 + 4 = 10$

63

Heart-shaped Box

Draw the correct number of chocolates in each box.

10   14

Draw 3 more chocolates in each box. Then write how many.

_14_   _15_

_8_

_9_   _18_

64

Yummy Tummy!

George has a tummy ache. Circle healthy snacks for George.

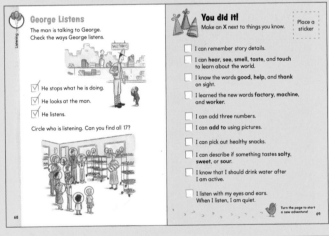

65

Taste It!

George can taste to learn if something is sweet, sour, or salty. Draw a line to a snack with the same taste.

It's sweet!

It's sour!

It's salty!

My favorite food is _Answers will vary._

It tastes (Circle one.)

66

At Work and Play

George loses water from his body when he **breathes** and **sweats**. Help George replace the water he lost. Draw a silly straw from the drink to George.

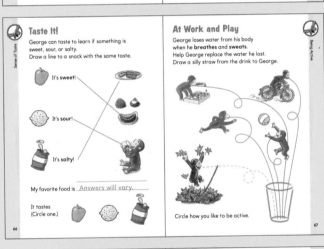

Circle how you like to be active.

67

George Listens

The man is talking to George. Check the ways George listens.

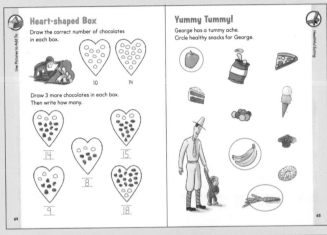

☑ He stops what he is doing.

☑ He looks at the man.

☑ He listens.

Circle who is listening. Can you find all 17?

68

You did it!

Make an X next to things you know.

Place a sticker

☐ I can remember story details.

☐ I can **hear, see, smell, taste, and touch** to learn about the world.

☐ I know the words **good, help,** and **thank** on sight.

☐ I learned the new words **factory, machine,** and **worker**.

☐ I can add three numbers.

☐ I can **add to** using pictures.

☐ I can pick out healthy snacks.

☐ I can describe if something tastes **salty, sweet,** or **sour**.

☐ I know that I should drink water after I am active.

☐ I listen with my eyes and ears. When I listen, I am quiet.

Turn the page to start a new adventure!

69

Double Feature

A movie poster can tell you about the story. Which story is made-up? Circle the clue.

Fossil Finder!

A story about real life has **facts**.

George and the Giant Dog

A made-up story is **fiction**.

Read about each story. Make an X next to stories about **real life**.

☒ A family takes a trip together.

☐ A dinosaur goes to school.

☒ A mother lion takes care of her cub.

☐ A dog wins a gold medal at the Olympics.

☒ A monkey grows up in the jungle.

78

Let's Pretend

Change each sentence from fact to fiction. Replace the underlined words with your own words.

Fact. George rode the bus to the city.

Fiction. George rode the bus to the _moon_!

Fact. The dogs ran to the park.

Fiction. The dogs _Sample answer: flew_ to the park!

Fact. George saw a duck outside his window.

Fiction. George saw a _Sample answer: dinosaur_ outside his window!

79

Two Tickets, Please!

Add –s to each word to show more than one.

ticket _tickets_

dinosaur _dinosaurs_

monkey _monkeys_

hat _hats_

bucket _buckets_ of popcorn!

Find words that mean more than one. Color in those tickets.

show   drink   movies   straws   screen   stars   seals   lights

80

More, Please!

George wants more than one. Rewrite each word to mean more than one. Add –s or –es.

snack _s_   box _es_

dish _es_   kiss _es_

lunch _es_   dime _s_

George wants two _Sample answer: donuts_ Draw them.

Sample drawing: 2 donuts

You can add –s to most words to show more than one. Add –es if the word ends with s, x, ch or sh.

81

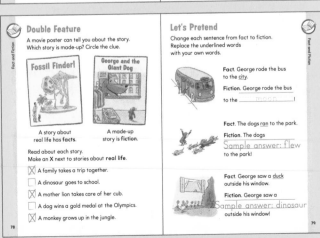
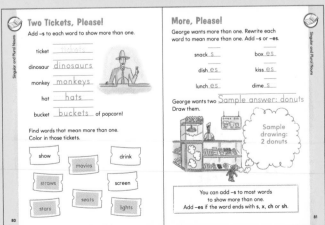

George in the Movies

George is going to be a movie star! Write the correct words to find out what happened.

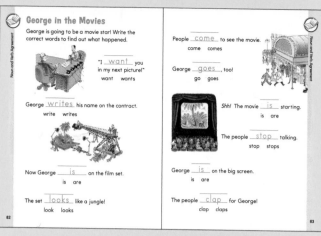

"I __want__ you in my next picture!"
want wants

George __writes__ his name on the contract.
write writes

Now George __is__ on the film set.
is are

The set __looks__ like a jungle!
look looks

82

People __come__ to see the movie.
come comes

George __goes__, too!
go goes

Shh! The movie __is__ starting.
is are

The people __stop__ talking.
stop stops

George __is__ on the big screen.
is are

The people __clap__ for George!
clap claps

83

Cowboy George

George dreams that he is in a cowboy movie. Find each word in the pictures. Then color it in.

all big him see has you

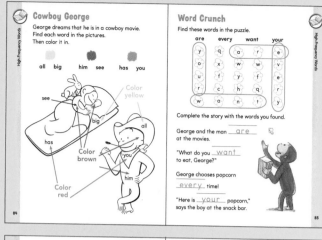

see
big
has
Color yellow
Color brown
you
him
Color red
all

84

Word Crunch

Find these words in the puzzle.

are every want your

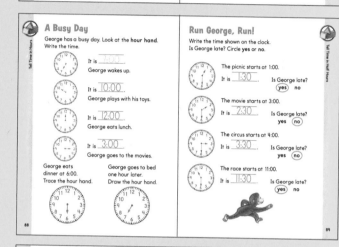

Complete the story with the words you found.

George and the man __are__ at the movies.

"What do you __want__ to eat, George?"

George chooses popcorn __every__ time!

"Here is __your__ popcorn," says the boy at the snack bar.

85

Pop! Pop! Pop!

George has five pieces of popcorn. Count the popcorn in each group. Write the numbers.

$3 + 2 = 5$ $2 + 3 = 5$

$4 + 1 = 5$ $1 + 4 = 5$

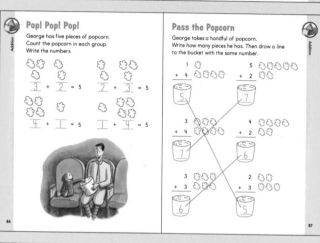

86

Pass the Popcorn

George takes a handful of popcorn. Write how many pieces he has. Then draw a line to the bucket with the same number.

1
+ 4
__5__

5
__5__

3
+ 4
__7__

7
__7__

3
+ 3
__6__

6

2
+ 3
__5__

4
__4__

2
+ 3
__5__

5

87

A Busy Day

George has a busy day. Look at the **hour hand**. Write the time.

It is __7:00__
George wakes up.

It is __10:00__
George plays with his toys.

It is __12:00__
George eats lunch.

It is __3:00__
George goes to the movies.

George eats dinner at 6:00. Trace the hour hand.

George goes to bed one hour later. Draw the hour hand.

88

Run George, Run!

Write the time shown on the clock. Is George late? Circle yes or no.

The picnic starts at 1:00.
It is __1:30__   Is George late? (yes) no

The movie starts at 3:00.
It is __2:30__   Is George late? yes (no)

The circus starts at 4:00.
It is __3:30__   Is George late? yes (no)

The race starts at 11:00.
It is __11:30__   Is George late? (yes) no

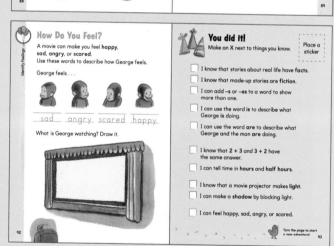

89

Hand Shadows

George is at the movies. It is dark. Then the movie starts.

Look at the picture. Circle where the light comes from.

George blocks the light with his hands. Which shadow did he make? Draw a line.

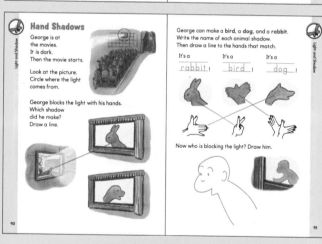

90

George can make a **bird**, a **dog**, and a **rabbit**. Write the name of each animal shadow. Then draw a line to the hands that match.

It's a __rabbit__   It's a __bird__   It's a __dog__

Now who is blocking the light? Draw him.

91

How Do You Feel?

A movie can make you feel **happy**, **sad**, **angry**, or **scared**. Use these words to describe how George feels.

George feels . . .

__sad__ __angry__ __scared__ __happy__

What is George watching? Draw it.

92

You did it!

Make an X next to things you know.

Place a sticker

☐ I know that stories about real life have **facts**.
☐ I know that made-up stories are **fiction**.
☐ I can add –s or –es to a word to show more than one.
☐ I can use the word **is** to describe what George is doing.
☐ I can use the word **are** to describe what George and the man **are** doing.
☐ I know that 2 + 3 and 3 + 2 have the same answer.
☐ I can tell time in **hours** and **half hours**.
☐ I know that a movie projector makes **light**.
☐ I can make a **shadow** by blocking light.
☐ I can feel happy, sad, angry, or scared.

Turn the page to start a new adventure!
93

Clap to It!

Clap to count the number of beats. Say each word. Then write the number.

wheel __1__
beat __1__

wheelchair __2__
beats __1__

medicine __3__
nurse __1__
scale __1__
water __2__
Sip! __1__
cabinet __3__
chair __1__

102

In the Playroom

Say each word.

Draw a line under words with one beat. Draw two lines under words with two beats.

table
puppets
book
paint
wagon
chair

Can you find something that has four beats? Circle it!

103

There's a Problem

Look at the picture. Who knows that there is a problem? Circle them.

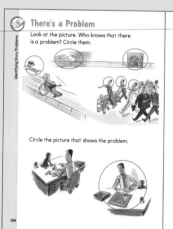

Circle the picture that shows the problem.

104

What's Wrong, George?

Tell what is wrong with George. Choose the best word to complete each sentence.

George's __tummy__ hurts.
foot tummy

He feels __sick__
angry sick

He does not want to __eat__
eat read

Circle the picture that can explain why George has a tummy ache. Then write to tell what happened.

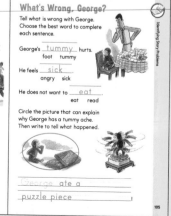

__George ate a__
__puzzle piece__

105

Answers, pp. 82–105

Doctor Visit

George went to the doctor.
Choose the best word
to complete each sentence.

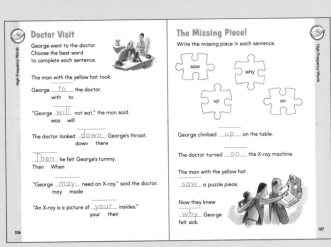

The man with the yellow hat took

George __to__ the doctor.
with **to**

"George __will__ not eat," the man said.
was **will**

The doctor looked __down__ George's throat.
down there

__Then__ he felt George's tummy.
Then When

"George __may__ need an X-ray," said the doctor.
may made

"An X-ray is a picture of __your__ insides."
your their

106

The Missing Piece!

Write the missing piece in each sentence.

saw
why
up
on

George climbed __up__ on the table.

The doctor turned __on__ the X-ray machine.

The man with the yellow hat
__saw__ a puzzle piece.

Now they knew
__why__ George
felt sick.

107

Puppet Show

George puts on a puppet show
for the children.

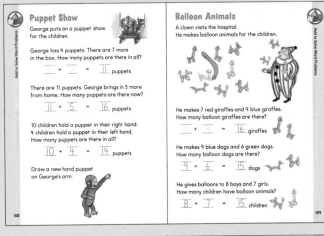

George has 4 puppets. There are 7 more
in the box. How many puppets are there in all?

4 + 7 = 11 puppets

There are 11 puppets. George brings in 5 more
from home. How many puppets are there now?

11 + 5 = 16 puppets

10 children hold a puppet in their right hand.
4 children hold a puppet in their left hand.
How many puppets are there in all?

10 + 4 = 14 puppets

Draw a new hand puppet
on George's arm.

108

Balloon Animals

A clown visits the hospital.
He makes balloon animals for the children.

He makes 7 red giraffes and 9 blue giraffes.
How many balloon giraffes are there?

7 + 9 = 16 giraffes

He makes 9 blue dogs and 6 green dogs.
How many balloon dogs are there?

9 + 6 = 15 dogs

He gives balloons to 8 boys and 7 girls.
How many children have balloon animals?

8 + 7 = 15 children

109

Balloons

Help George count the balloons. Find 10 less
and 10 more than the middle number.

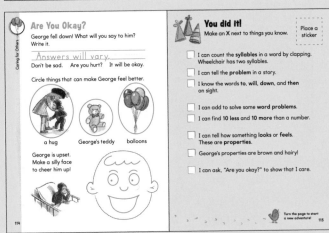

10 less		10 more
1	11	21
4	14	24
19	29	39
2	12	22
16	26	36

110

Flowers

Now help George count the flowers in the gift shop.
Find 10 less or 10 more to fill in the blanks.

10 less		10 more
1	11	21
3	13	23
10	20	30
24	34	44
94	104	114

Show 10 less. Make an X on 10 flowers.

There are 8 flowers left.

111

Twenty Questions

Write one word that tells about both pictures.

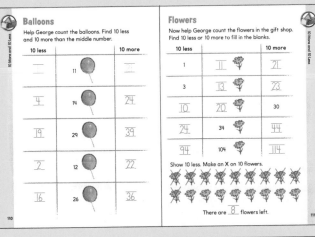

Both are __crunchy__

Both are __yellow__

Both are __sweet__

Both are __round__

112

George is thinking of a picture on this page.
It is hard and yellow.
Can you figure out what it is?

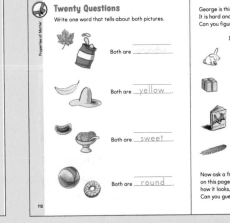

It is a __book__

Now ask a friend to think of a picture
on this page. Ask **yes** or **no** questions about
how it looks, feels, sounds, or tastes.
Can you guess what it is?

113

Are You Okay?

George fell down! What will you say to him?
Write it.

__Answers will vary.__

Don't be sad.   Are you hurt?   It will be okay.

Circle things that can make George feel better.

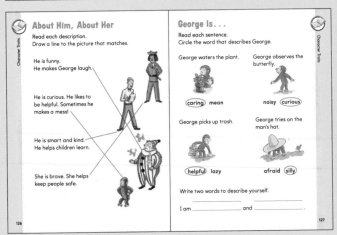

a hug   George's teddy   balloons

George is upset.
Make a silly face
to cheer him up!

114

You did it!

Make an X next to things you know.

Place a sticker

☐ I can count the **syllables** in a word by clapping.
Wheelchair has two syllables.

☐ I can tell the **problem** in a story.

☐ I know the words **to, will, down,** and **then**
on sight.

☐ I can add to solve some **word problems.**

☐ I can find **10 less** and **10 more** than a number.

☐ I can tell how something **looks** or **feels.**
These are **properties.**

☐ George's **properties** are brown and hairy!

☐ I can ask, "Are you okay?" to show that I care.

Turn the page to start
a new adventure!

115

Easy as 1, 2, 3

George learned how to recycle.
Write 1, 2, and 3 to put the story in order.

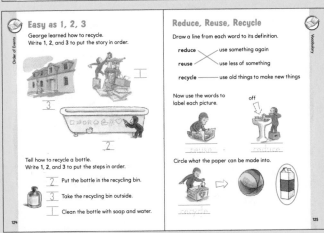

1

3

2

Tell how to recycle a bottle.
Write 1, 2, and 3 to put the steps in order.

2 Put the bottle in the recycling bin.

3 Take the recycling bin outside.

1 Clean the bottle with soap and water.

124

Reduce, Reuse, Recycle

Draw a line from each word to its definition.

reduce — use something again
reuse — use less of something
recycle — use old things to make new things

Now use the words to
label each picture.

off

__reuse__   __reduce__

Circle what the paper can be made into.

__recycle__

125

About Him, About Her

Read each description.
Draw a line to the picture that matches.

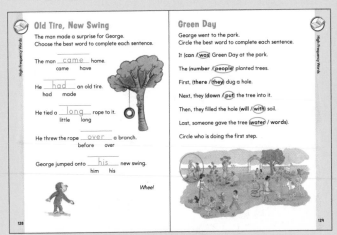

He is funny.
He makes George laugh.

He is curious. He likes to
be helpful. Sometimes he
makes a mess!

He is smart and kind.
He helps children learn.

She is brave. She helps
keep people safe.

126

George Is . . .

Read each sentence.
Circle the word that describes George.

George waters the plant.

(caring)   mean

George picks up trash.

(helpful)   lazy

George observes the butterfly.

noisy   (curious)

George tries on the man's hat.

afraid   (silly)

Write two words to describe yourself.

I am _____ and _____.

127

Old Tire, New Swing

The man made a surprise for George.
Choose the best word to complete each sentence.

The man __came__ home.
came have

He __had__ an old tire.
had made

He tied a __long__ rope to it.
little **long**

He threw the rope __over__ a branch.
before **over**

George jumped onto __his__ new swing.
him **his**

Whee!

128

Green Day

George went to the park.
Circle the best word to complete each sentence.

It (can / (was)) Green Day at the park.

The (number / (people)) planted trees.

First, (there / (they)) dug a hole.

Next, they (down / (put)) the tree into it.

Then, they filled the hole (will / (with)) soil.

Last, someone gave the tree ((water) / words).

Circle who is doing the first step.

129

Answers, pp. 106-129

311

Reuse or Recycle?

Can each item be reused or recycled? Add it to the correct list.

reuse	recycle
shoes	carton
hat	box
toy	can

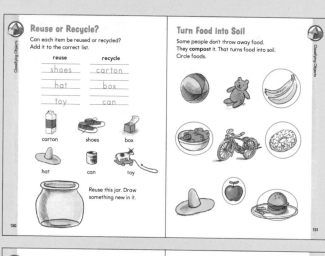

carton   shoes   box

hat   can   toy

Reuse this jar. Draw something new in it.

130

Turn Food into Soil

Some people don't throw away food. They **compost** it. That turns food into soil. Circle foods.

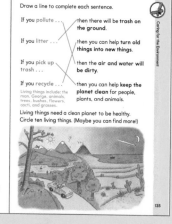

131

Can Collection

George collected cans to recycle.

Thursday	🥫🥫🥫🥫
Friday	🥫🥫🥫🥫🥫🥫🥫
Saturday	🥫🥫🥫🥫🥫🥫🥫🥫🥫🥫

He collected **4** cans on Thursday.

He collected **7** cans on Friday.

He collected **19** cans in all.

He collected the most cans on **Saturday**.

George collected 3 fewer cans on Sunday than on Saturday. Draw how many cans he collected on Sunday.

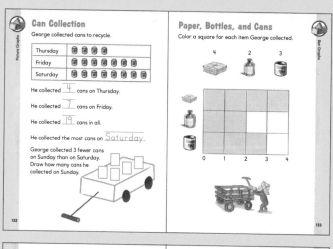

132

Paper, Bottles, and Cans

Color a square for each item George collected.

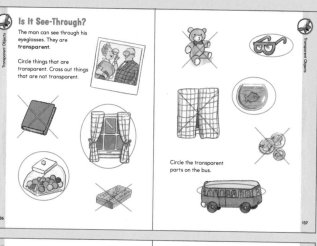

0   1   2   3   4

133

Keep It Clean

George helps keep land, water, and air clean. Write **land**, **water**, or **air** to tell how.

George picks up trash.

This keeps the **land** clean.

George rides a bike.

This keeps the **air** clean.

George takes his toys home from the beach.

This keeps the **water** clean.

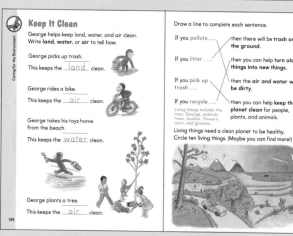

George plants a tree.

This keeps the **air** clean.

134

Draw a line to complete each sentence.

If you pollute . . . → then you can help turn old things into new things.

If you litter . . . → then there will be **trash on the ground.**

If you pick up trash . . . → then the air and water will **be dirty.**

If you recycle . . . → then you can help keep the **planet clean** for people, plants, and animals.

Living things include: the man, George, animals, trees, bushes, flowers, cacti, and grasses.

Living things need a clean planet to be healthy. Circle ten living things. (Maybe you can find more!)

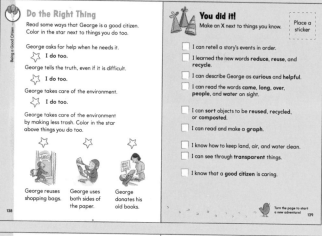

135

Is It See-Through?

The man can see through his eyeglasses. They are **transparent.**

Circle things that are transparent. Cross out things that are not transparent.

Circle the transparent parts on the bus.

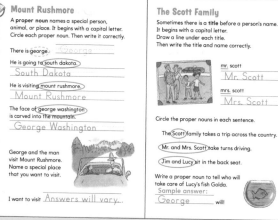

136

137

Do the Right Thing

Read some ways that George is a good citizen. Color in the star next to things you do too.

George asks for help when he needs it.

☆ **I do too.**

George tells the truth, even if it is difficult.

☆ **I do too.**

George takes care of the environment.

☆ **I do too.**

George takes care of the environment by making less trash. Color in the star above things you do too.

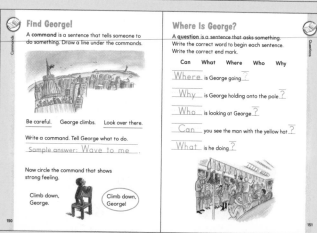

☆ George reuses shopping bags.

☆ George uses both sides of the paper.

☆ George donates his old books.

138

You did it!

Make an X next to things you know.

☐ Place a sticker

☐ I can retell a story's events in order.

☐ I learned the new words **reduce**, **reuse**, and **recycle**.

☐ I can describe George as **curious** and **helpful**.

☐ I can read the words **came**, **long**, **over**, **people**, and **water** on sight.

☐ I can **sort** objects to be **reused**, **recycled**, or **composted**.

☐ I can read and make a **graph**.

☐ I know how to keep land, air, and water clean.

☐ I can see through **transparent** things.

☐ I know that a **good citizen** is caring.

🐤 Turn the page to start a new adventure!

139

Mount Rushmore

A **proper noun** names a special person, animal, or place. It begins with a capital letter. Circle each proper noun. Then write it correctly.

There is ~~george~~ (George).

George

He is going to ~~south dakota~~.

South Dakota

He is visiting ~~mount rushmore~~.

Mount Rushmore

The face of ~~george washington~~ is carved into the mountain.

George Washington

George and the man visit Mount Rushmore. Name a special place that you want to visit.

I want to visit **Answers will vary.**

148

The Scott Family

Sometimes there is a **title** before a person's name. It begins with a capital letter. Draw a line under each title. Then write the title and name correctly.

mr. scott

Mr. Scott

mrs. scott

Mrs. Scott

Circle the proper nouns in each sentence.

The (Scott) family takes a trip across the country.

(Mr.) and (Mrs. Scott) take turns driving.

(Jim and Lucy) sit in the back seat.

Write a proper noun to tell who will take care of Lucy's fish Golda.

Sample answer: **George** will!

149

Find George!

A **command** is a sentence that tells someone to do something. Draw a line under the commands.

Be careful.   George climbs.   Look over there.

Write a command. Tell George what to do.

Sample answer: **Wave to me.**

Now circle the command that shows strong feeling.

Climb down, George.   (Climb down, George!)

150

Where Is George?

A **question** is a sentence that asks something. Write the correct word to begin each sentence. Write the correct end mark.

Can   What   Where   Who   Why

Where is George going **?**

Why is George holding onto the pole **?**

Who is looking at George **?**

Can you see the man with the yellow hat **?**

What he is doing **?**

151

Big City

George and the man took a carriage ride. Add the correct suffix to each word.

-y   -ly   -ful

It was a snow **y** day.

Snowflakes fell soft **ly**.

It was peace **ful**.

The horse moved slow **ly**.

George felt joy **ful**.

Why do you think George felt joyful?

Sample answer: **He is with his friend**

152

What's Up, George?

George is at the museum. Write a **contraction** for the underlined words.

can't   He's   isn't   It's   There's

He is looking for the man.

He's

George cannot see him.

can't

The man is not below.

isn't

There is the man!

There's

The man says, "It is time to go home."

It's

Goodbye, Big City!

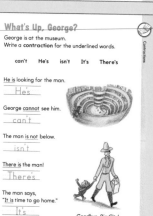

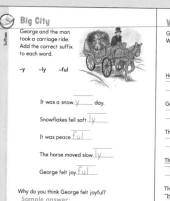

153

Answers, pp. 130-153

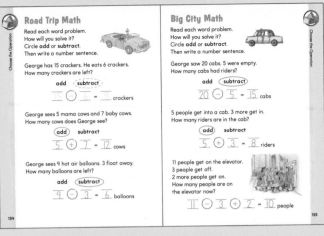

Road Trip Math

Read each word problem.
How will you solve it?
Circle **add** or **subtract**.
Then write a number sentence.

George has 15 crackers. He eats 6 crackers.
How many crackers are left?

add (subtract)

$15 - 6 = 9$ crackers

George sees 5 mama cows and 7 baby cows.
How many cows does George see?

(add) subtract

$5 + 7 = 12$ cows

George sees 9 hot air balloons. 3 float away.
How many balloons are left?

add (subtract)

$9 - 3 = 6$ balloons

154

Big City Math

Read each word problem.
How will you solve it?
Circle **add** or **subtract**.
Then write a number sentence.

George saw 20 cabs. 5 were empty.
How many cabs had riders?

add (subtract)

$20 - 5 = 15$ cabs

5 people get into a cab. 3 more get in.
How many riders are in the cab?

(add) subtract

$5 + 3 = 8$ riders

11 people get on the elevator.
3 people get off.
2 more people get on.
How many people are on
the elevator now?

$11 - 3 + 2 = 10$ people

155

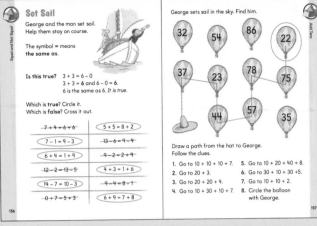

Set Sail

George and the man set sail.
Help them stay on course.

The symbol = means
the same as.

Is this true? 3 + 3 = 6 – 0
3 + 3 = **6** and 6 – 0 = 6.
6 is the same as 6. *It is true.*

Which is **true**? Circle it.
Which is **false**? Cross it out.

~~–7 + 4 = 6 + 6~~   (5 + 5 = 8 + 2)
(7 – 1 = 9 – 3)   ~~–13 – 6 = 9 – 4~~
(6 + 4 = 1 + 9)   ~~–9 – 2 = 2 + 9~~
~~–12 – 2 = 13 – 5~~   (4 + 3 = 1 + 6)
(14 – 7 = 10 – 3)   ~~–9 – 4 = 8 – 1~~
~~–0 + 7 = 5 + 3~~   (6 + 9 = 7 + 8)

156

George sets sail in the sky. Find him.

32   54   86   22
37   23   78   75
44   57   35

Draw a path from the hat to George.
Follow the clues.

1. Go to 10 + 10 + 7.
2. Go to 20 + 3.
3. Go to 20 + 20 + 4.
4. Go to 10 + 30 + 10 + 7.
5. Go to 10 + 20 + 40 + 8.
6. Go to 30 + 10 + 30 +5.
7. Go to 10 + 10 + 2.
8. Circle the balloon
   with George.

157

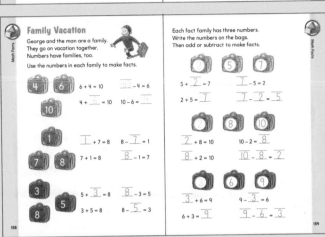

Family Vacation

George and the man are a family.
They go on vacation together.
Numbers have families, too.
Use the numbers in each family to make facts.

4 6
6 + 4 = 10 $10 – 4 = 6$
4 + 6 = 10   10 – 6 = 4

10

1 7
1 + 7 = 8   8 – 1 = 7
7 + 1 = 8 8 – 1 = 7

8

3 5
5 + 3 = 8 8 – 3 = 5
3 + 5 = 8   8 – 5 = 3

8

158

Each fact family has three numbers.
Write the numbers on the bags.
Then add or subtract to make facts.

5 7
5 + 2 = 7 7 – 5 = 2
2 + 5 = 7 7 – 2 = 5

8 10
2 + 8 = 10   10 – 2 = 8
8 + 2 = 10 10 – 8 = 2

3 9
3 + 6 = 9   9 – 3 = 6
6 + 3 = 9 9 – 6 = 3

159

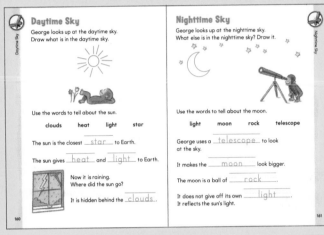

Daytime Sky

George looks up at the daytime sky.
Draw what is in the daytime sky.

Use the words to tell about the sun.

clouds   heat   light   star

The sun is the closest ___star___ to Earth.

The sun gives ___heat___ and ___light___ to Earth.

Now it is raining.
Where did the sun go?

It is hidden behind the ___clouds___.

160

Nighttime Sky

George looks up at the nighttime sky.
What else is in the nighttime sky? Draw it.

Use the words to tell about the moon.

light   moon   rock   telescope

George uses a ___telescope___ to look
at the sky.

It makes the ___moon___ look bigger.

The moon is a ball of ___rock___.

It does not give off its own ___light___.
It reflects the sun's light.

161

Have a Safe Trip!

Tell George how to stay safe on a trip.
Make an X next to what you would do.

If I am in a car . . .
[X] I wear a seatbelt.   [ ] I do not wear a seatbelt.

If I am in a boat . . .
[X] I wear a life jacket.   [ ] I sit on my life jacket.

If I want to see something new . . .
[ ] I walk away from my family.
[X] I stay with my family.
[X] I never go with people who say
    they know my family.

Draw a
life jacket
on George.
Then draw
yourself on
the boat.

162

You did it!

Make an X next to things you know.

[Place a sticker]

[ ] I know that a **proper noun** names a special
    person or place. It begins with a capital letter.

[ ] A **command** is a sentence that tells someone
    to do something.

[ ] A **question** is a sentence that asks something.

[ ] I can use an apostrophe to push two words
    together. It's easy.

[ ] I can turn a word problem into a number
    sentence.

[ ] I know that = means **the same as.**

[ ] I can make facts about **number families.**

[ ] I know the **sun** gives light and heat to Earth.

[ ] I know the **moon** does not give light.

[ ] I can make good choices.

Turn the page to start
a new adventure!

163

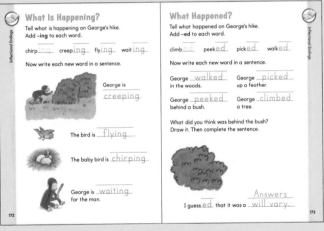

What Is Happening?

Tell what is happening on George's hike.
Add **-ing** to each word.

chirp**ing**   creep**ing**   fly**ing**   wait**ing**

Now write each new word in a sentence.

George is
___creeping___.

The bird is ___flying___.

The baby bird is ___chirping___.

George is ___waiting___
for the man.

172

What Happened?

Tell what happened on George's hike.
Add **-ed** to each word.

climb**ed**   peek**ed**   pick**ed**   walk**ed**

Now write each new word in a sentence.

George ___walked___   George ___picked___
in the woods.   up a feather.

George ___peeked___   George ___climbed___
behind a bush.   a tree.

What did you think was behind the bush?
Draw it. Then complete the sentence.

I guess**ed** that it was a ___Answers
                              will vary___.

173

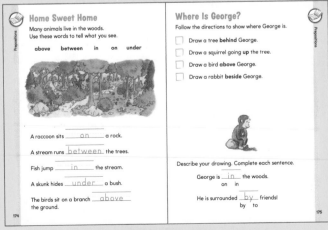

Home Sweet Home

Many animals live in the woods.
Use these words to tell what you see.

above   between   in   on   under

A raccoon sits ___on___ a rock.

A stream runs ___between___ the trees.

Fish jump ___in___ the stream.

A skunk hides ___under___ a bush.

The birds sit on a branch ___above___
the ground.

174

Where Is George?

Follow the directions to show where George is.

[ ] Draw a tree **behind** George.
[ ] Draw a squirrel going **up** the tree.
[ ] Draw a bird **above** George.
[ ] Draw a rabbit **beside** George.

Describe your drawing. Complete each sentence.

George is ___in___ the woods.
                on in

He is surrounded ___by___ friends!
                  by to

175

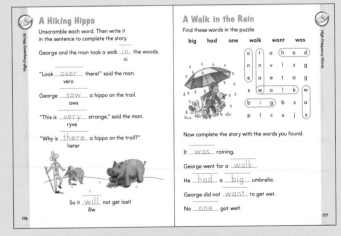

A Hiking Hippo

Unscramble each word. Then write it
in the sentence to complete the story.

George and the man took a walk ___in___ the woods.
                                   ni

"Look ___over___ there!" said the man.
       vero

George ___saw___ a hippo on the trail.
        aws

"This is ___very___ strange," said the man.
          ryve

"Why is ___there___ a hippo on the trail?"
         heter

So it ___will___ not get lost!
       illw

176

A Walk in the Rain

Find these words in the puzzle.

big   had   one   walk   want   was

a	t	a	h	a	d
n	n	v	l	z	g
e	a	e	t	a	g
s	w	a	l	k	w
b	i	g	b	s	a
p	l	c	u	j	s

(circled: h a d; w a l k; b i g)

Now complete the story with the words you found.

It ___was___ raining.

George went for a ___walk___.

He ___had___ a ___big___ umbrella.

George did not ___want___ to get wet.

No ___one___ got wet!

177

Feather Measure

Use the feather to measure.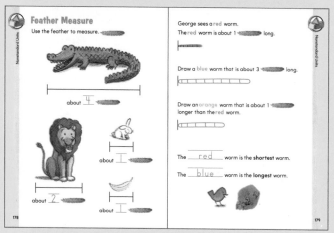

about 4

about 1

about 2

about 1

George sees a red worm.
The red worm is about 1 _____ long.

Draw a blue worm that is about 3 _____ long.

Draw an orange worm that is about 1 _____ longer than the red worm.

The _red_ worm is the **shortest** worm.

The _blue_ worm is the **longest** worm.

178

179

Pack a Snack

George and the man pack snacks for the hike.

Each [ ] = 1 ten

Draw bags to show how many tens there are.
Add the tens. Then write a number sentence.

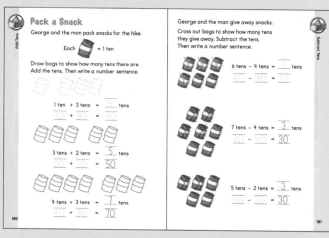

1 ten + 3 tens = _3_ tens
10 + 30 = 40

3 tens + 2 tens = _5_ tens
30 + 20 = 50

4 tens + 3 tens = _7_ tens
40 + 30 = 70

George and the man give away snacks.
Cross out bags to show how many tens
they give away. Subtract the tens.
Then write a number sentence.

6 tens – 4 tens = _2_ tens
60 – 40 = 20

7 tens – 4 tens = _3_ tens
70 – 40 = 30

5 tens – 2 tens = _3_ tens
50 – 20 = 30

180

181

Up, Down, All Around

The bird lives in the woods. That is where
it can get what it needs to survive.

It needs **food.**   It needs **shelter.**

Write one thing each animal needs.
Can it find what it needs in the woods?
Circle yes or no.

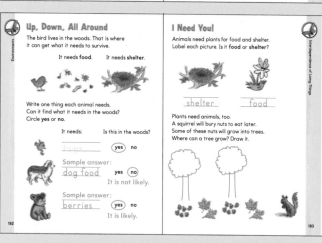

It needs: Is this in the woods?

bugs   (yes) no

Sample answer:
dog food   yes (no)
It is not likely.

Sample answer:
berries   (yes) no
It is likely.

I Need You!

Animals need plants for food and shelter.
Label each picture. Is it **food** or **shelter**?

shelter   _food_

Plants need animals, too.
A squirrel will bury nuts to eat later.
Some of these nuts will grow into trees.
Where can a tree grow? Draw it.

182

183

A Walk in the Woods

George goes on a hike. Color in the leaf
next to things George should do.

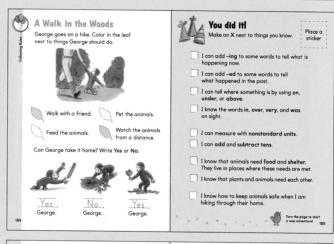

🍃 Walk with a friend.   Pet the animals.

🍃 Feed the animals.   🍃 Watch the animals
from a distance.

Can George take it home? Write **Yes** or **No.**

Yes,   _No_,   _Yes_,
George.   George.   George.

You did it!

Make an X next to things you know.

Place a sticker

☐ I can add –**ing** to some words to tell what is
happening now.

☐ I can add –**ed** to some words to tell
what happened in the past.

☐ I can tell where something is by using **on,
under,** or **above.**

☐ I know the words **in, over, very,** and **was**
on sight.

☐ I can measure with **nonstandard** units.

☐ I can **add** and **subtract** tens.

☐ I know that animals need **food** and **shelter.**
They live in places where these needs are met.

☐ I know that plants and animals need each other.

☐ I know how to keep animals safe when I am
hiking through their home.

Turn the page to start
a new adventure!

184

185

Pepperoni, Please!

Which toppings does each child want?
Trace the joining words to find out.
Then circle the toppings.

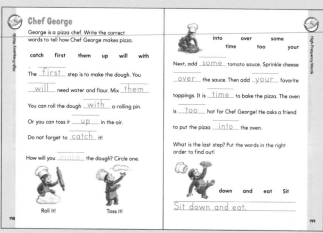

wants mushrooms _and_ sauce.

mushrooms pepperoni peppers sauce

wants mushrooms _or_ pepperoni.

mushrooms pepperoni peppers sauce

wants peppers _and_ pepperoni. Draw it.

mushrooms   peppers

pepperoni   sauce

Super Star Pizza

What toppings do you like on your pizza?
Write them below.

I like _____ _and_ _____

I like _____ _but_ I don't

like _____

Draw toppings on your pizza.
Then tell about your pizza.

My pizza has _____ and _____

but it does not have _____

194

195

The Best Word

Which word describes the picture better?
Write it.

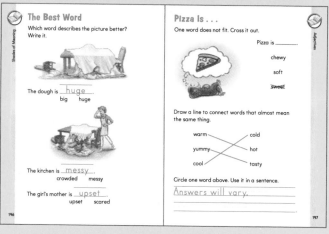

The dough is _huge_
big huge

The kitchen is _messy_
crowded messy

The girl's mother is _upset_
upset scared

Pizza Is . . .

One word does not fit. Cross it out.

Pizza is _____

chewy

soft

~~sweet~~

Draw a line to connect words that almost mean
the same thing.

warm ⟍⟋ cold
yummy ⤬ hot
cool ⟋⟍ tasty

Circle one word above. Use it in a sentence.

Answers will vary.

196

197

Chef George

George is a pizza chef. Write the correct
words to tell how Chef George makes pizza.

catch first them up will with

The _first_ step is to make the dough. You

will need water and flour. Mix _them_

You can roll the dough _with_ a rolling pin.

Or you can toss it _up_ in the air.

Do not forget to _catch_ it!

How will you _make_ the dough? Circle one.

Roll it!   Toss it!

---

into over some
time too your

Next, add _some_ tomato sauce. Sprinkle cheese

over the sauce. Then add _your_ favorite

toppings. It is _time_ to bake the pizza. The oven

is _too_ hot for Chef George! He asks a friend

to put the pizza _into_ the oven.

What is the last step? Put the words in the right
order to find out!

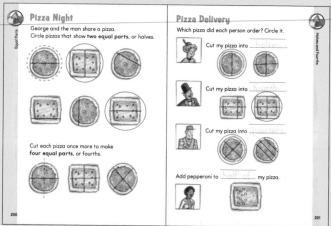

down and eat Sit

Sit down and eat.

198

199

Pizza Night

George and the man share a pizza.
Circle pizzas that show **two equal parts,** or halves.

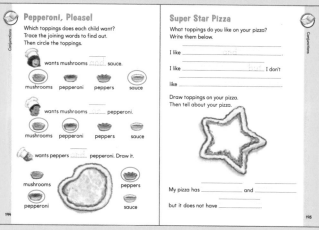

Cut each pizza once more to make
four equal parts, or fourths.

Pizza Delivery

Which pizza did each person order? Circle it.

Cut my pizza into _halves_

Cut my pizza into _fourths_

Cut my pizza into _quarters_

Add pepperoni to _half of_ my pizza.

200

201

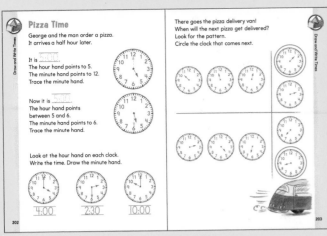

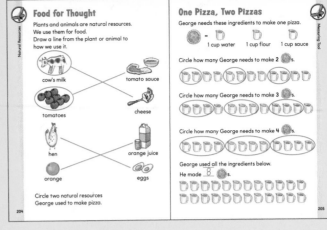

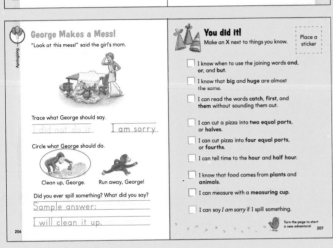

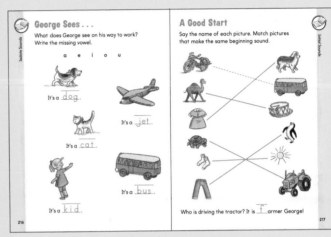

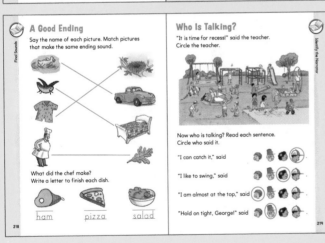

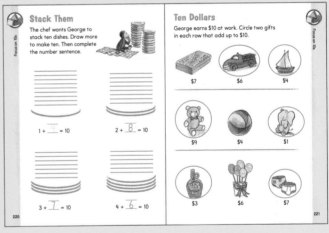

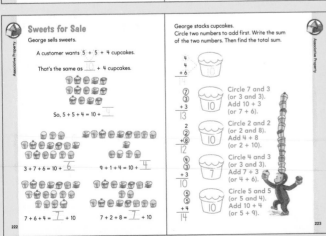

Answers, pp. 202-225

315

Good Job!

A chore is a small job. Do you help with these chores? Circle yes or no.

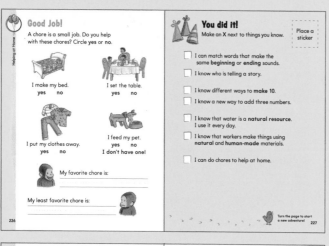

I make my bed.
yes   no

I set the table.
yes   no

I put my clothes away.
yes   no

I feed my pet.
yes   no
I don't have one!

My favorite chore is:
_____

My least favorite chore is:
_____

226

You did it!

Make an X next to things you know.

Place a sticker

☐ I can match words that make the same **beginning** or **ending** sounds.

☐ I know who is telling a story.

☐ I know different ways to **make 10**.

☐ I know a new way to add three numbers.

☐ I know that water is a **natural resource**. I use it every day.

☐ I know that workers make things using **natural** and **human-made** materials.

☐ I can do chores to help at home.

Turn the page to start a new adventure!
227

A Special Day

George wants to remember special days. Show him how to write each date correctly.

The boy had a birthday party on may 20 2014.
May 20, 2014

The dog had puppies on august 1 2014.
August 1, 2014

The toy store opened on march 23 2012.
March 23, 2012

Draw yourself and a friend.

This is me.

This is _____

I was born on

(He / She) was born on

238

George's Friend

A possessive noun tells who owns something.

It is _George's_ friend!

Use the words to complete each sentence.

dog's
elephant's
frog's
girl's
tree's

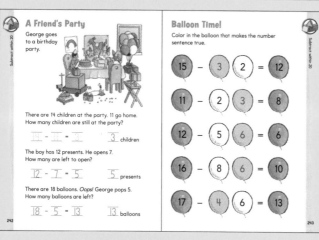

The _girl's_ shoes are blue.

The _dog's_ tail is long.

The _frog's_ legs are green.

The _tree's_ trunk is brown.

But the _elephant's_ trunk is gray!

239

A Friend's Party

George goes to a birthday party.

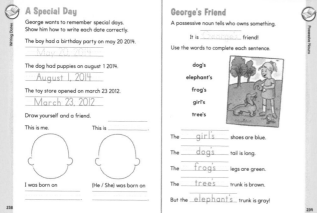

There are 14 children at the party. 11 go home. How many children are still at the party?

_14_ - _11_ = _3_   _3_ children

The boy has 12 presents. He opens 7. How many are left to open?

_12_ - _7_ = _5_   _5_ presents

There are 18 balloons. Oops! George pops 5. How many balloons are left?

_18_ - _5_ = _13_   _13_ balloons

242

Balloon Time!

Color in the balloon that makes the number sentence true.

15 - 3   **2**   = 12

11 - 2   **3**   = 8

12 - 5   **6**   = 6

16 - 8   **6**   = 10

17 - 4   **6**   = 13

243

Birthday Treats

George eats hot and cold food at the birthday party.

Temperature is the measure of how hot or cold something is.

Is it hot or cold? Circle one.

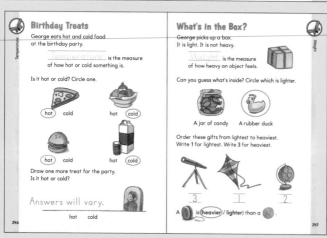

hot cold

hot **cold**

hot cold

hot **cold**

Draw one more treat for the party. Is it hot or cold?

Answers will vary.

hot cold

246

What's in the Box?

George picks up a box. It is light. It is not heavy.

Weight is the measure of how heavy an object feels.

Can you guess what's inside? Circle which is lighter.

A jar of candy   A rubber duck

Order these gifts from lightest to heaviest. Write 1 for lightest. Write 3 for heaviest.

_3_   _1_   _2_

A _1_ is (**heavier** / lighter) than a _2_.
hot cold

247

A Fun Party

Describe the party. Write the best adjective to describe each noun.

green   happy   red   soft

George saw a _green_ present.

It had a _red_ bow.

George opened it.

It was a _soft_ teddy bear.

George was a _happy_ monkey!

Color in George's party hat. Then describe it.

It's a _Answers will vary._ party hat.

236

Presents!

George opened his presents. The children played with them. Write an adjective to describe each one.

green   loud   round   striped   yellow

yellow duck

round ball

green dinosaur

loud horn

striped puppet

237

Birthday Cake

George makes a cake. Write the best word to complete each sentence.

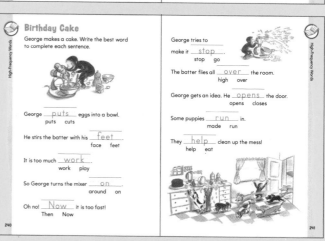

George _puts_ eggs into a bowl.
puts   cuts

He stirs the batter with his _feet_.
face   feet

It is too much _work_.
work   play

So George turns the mixer _on_.
around   on

Oh no! _Now_ it is too fast!
Then   Now

240

George tries to make it _stop_.
stop   go

The batter flies all _over_ the room.
high   over

George gets an idea. He _opens_ the door.
opens   closes

Some puppies _run_ in.
made   run

They _help_ clean up the mess!
help   eat

241

Greater Than

Compare the number of candles on each cake.

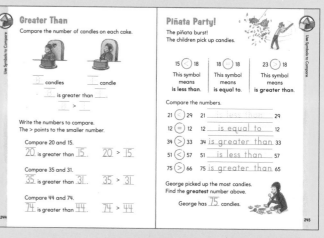

_3_ candles   _1_ candle

_3_ is greater than _1_.
_3_ > _1_

Write the numbers to compare. The > points to the smaller number.

Compare 20 and 15.
_20_ is greater than _15_   _20_ > _15_

Compare 35 and 31.
_35_ is greater than _31_   _35_ > _31_

Compare 44 and 74.
_74_ is greater than _44_   _74_ > _44_

244

Piñata Party!

The piñata burst! The children pick up candies.

15 **<** 18   18 **=** 18   23 **>** 18
This symbol means **is less than**.   This symbol means **is equal to**.   This symbol means **is greater than**.

Compare the numbers.

21 **<** 29   21 _is less than_ 29

12 **=** 12   12 _is equal to_ 12

34 **>** 33   34 _is greater than_ 33

51 **<** 57   51 _is less than_ 57

75 **>** 66   75 _is greater than_ 65

George picked up the most candies. Find the **greatest** number above.

George has _75_ candies.

245

How Kind!

George has kind friends.

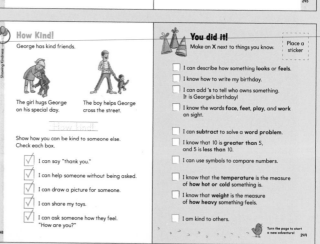

The girl hugs George on his special day.

The boy helps George cross the street.

How Kind!

Show how you can be kind to someone else. Check each box.

☑ I can say "thank you."

☑ I can help someone without being asked.

☑ I can draw a picture for someone.

☑ I can share my toys.

☑ I can ask someone how they feel. "How are you?"

248

You did it!

Make an X next to things you know.

Place a sticker

☐ I can describe how something **looks** or **feels**.

☐ I know how to write my birthday.

☐ I can add **'s** to tell who owns something. It is George's birthday!

☐ I know the words **face, feet, play,** and **work** on sight.

☐ I can **subtract** to solve a **word problem**.

☐ I know that 10 is **greater than** 5, and 5 is **less than** 10.

☐ I can use symbols to compare numbers.

☐ I know that the **temperature** is the measure of **how hot or cold** something is.

☐ I know that **weight** is the measure of **how heavy** something feels.

☐ I am kind to others.

Turn the page to start a new adventure!
249

Apples!

George visited a farm. Write the correct word to complete each sentence.

George **went** to the apple farm.
went   gone

He spent the day **outside**.
inside   outside

He climbed to the **top** of a tree.
top   behind

He **gave** an apple to the farmer.
gave   have

"Thank you, George," **she** said.
her   she

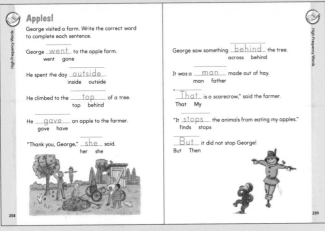

George saw something **behind** the tree.
across   behind

It was a **man** made out of hay.
man   father

"**That** is a scarecrow," said the farmer.
That   My

"It **stops** the animals from eating my apples."
finds   stops

But it did not stop George!
But   Then

258   259

Yesterday!

Tell what happened yesterday.
Circle the correct verb.
Then write the sentence.

George (**plays** / **played**) in the hay.
George played in the hay.

George (**picks** / **picked**) apples.
George picked apples.

George (**collects** / **collected**) eggs.
George collected eggs.

The chicks (**chirp** / **chirped**).
The chicks chirped.

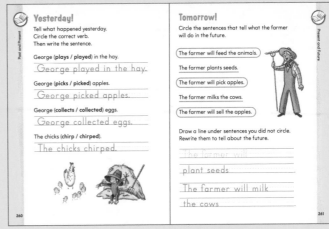

Tomorrow!

Circle the sentences that tell what the farmer will do in the future.

(The farmer will feed the animals.)
The farmer plants seeds.
(The farmer will pick apples.)
The farmer milks the cows.
(The farmer will sell the apples.)

Draw a line under sentences you did not circle. Rewrite them to tell about the future.

The farmer will
plant seeds
The farmer will milk
the cows

260   261

On the Farm

George counts the red and green apple trees at the farm.

Apple Trees		Total
trees	IIII	5
trees	IIII III	8

(Color it in.)
There are more 🍎 apple trees.

The farmer plants the trees in a pattern.
Complete the pattern in each row.

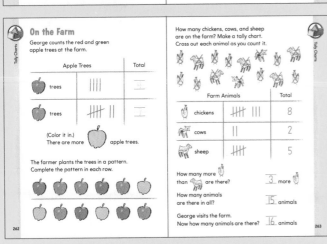

How many chickens, cows, and sheep are on the farm? Make a tally chart. Cross out each animal as you count it.

Farm Animals		Total
chickens	IIII III	8
cows	II	2
sheep	IIII	5

How many more 🐔 than 🐑 are there?   **3** more

How many animals are there in all?   **15** animals

George visits the farm.
Now how many animals are there?   **16** animals

262   263

Chicken Coop

George sees many shapes at the farm.
Color in the shape you see on the coop.

George holds a shape. Color it in.

Color in shapes that are both curved and closed.

Color in shapes with 4 sides.

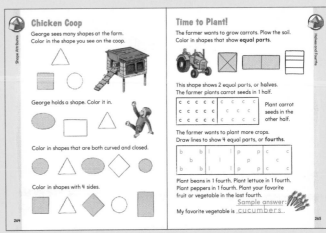

Time to Plant!

The farmer wants to grow carrots. Plow the soil.
Color in shapes that show **equal parts**.

This shape shows 2 equal parts, or **halves**.
The farmer plants carrot seeds in 1 half.

c c c c	c c c
c c c c	c c c
c c c c	c c c

Plant carrot seeds in the other half.

The farmer wants to plant more crops.
Draw lines to show 4 equal parts, or **fourths**.

| b b | l l | p p | c c |
| b b | l l | p p | c c |

Plant beans in 1 fourth. Plant lettuce in 1 fourth.
Plant peppers in 1 fourth. Plant your favorite fruit or vegetable in the last fourth.

Sample answer:
My favorite vegetable is **cucumbers**.

264   265

Growing Up

George needs room to grow. So do plants!
As a plant grows, its roots get bigger.
It grows more leaves.
Draw an adult plant.

seedling   adult plant
leaves
roots

Use the words to complete each plant fact.

stem   roots   water

The **roots** grow into the soil.

They take in **water**
that the plant needs.

A **stem** carries water to other plant parts.

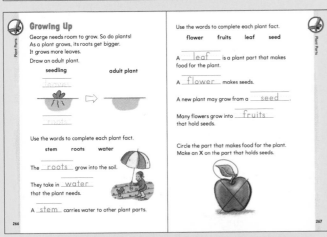

Use the words to complete each plant fact.

flower   fruits   leaf   seed

A **leaf** is a plant part that makes food for the plant.

A **flower** makes seeds.

A new plant may grow from a **seed**.

Many flowers grow into **fruits**
that hold seeds.

Circle the part that makes food for the plant.
Make an **X** on the part that holds seeds.

266   267

Farm to Tummy

People and animals use plants for food.

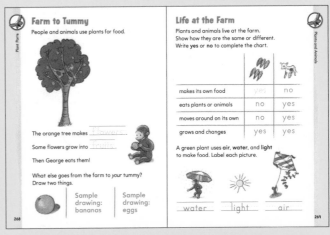

The orange tree makes **flowers**.
Some flowers grow into **fruit**.
Then George eats them!

What else goes from the farm to your tummy?
Draw two things.

Sample drawing: bananas   Sample drawing: eggs

Life at the Farm

Plants and animals live at the farm.
Show how they are the same or different.
Write **yes** or **no** to complete the chart.

	🌱	🐑
makes its own food	yes	no
eats plants or animals	no	yes
moves around on its own	no	yes
grows and changes	yes	yes

A green plant uses **air**, **water**, and **light** to make food. Label each picture.

water   **light**   **air**

268   269

Farm to Table Manners

Tell George how to use good table manners.
Circle the words.

(**Stand** / **Sit**) at the table.

Wash your hands (**before** / **after**) eating.

Take (**big** / **small**) bites.

(**Do not** / **Do**) play at the table.

Chew with your mouth (**closed** / **open**).

Eat with your (**fork** / **hands**).

What's for dinner? Set a place for George.
Then draw food on the plate.

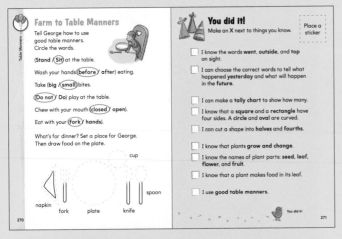

cup
napkin   fork   plate   knife   spoon

You did it!

Make an **X** next to things you know.

Place a sticker

☐ I know the words **went**, **outside**, and **top** on sight.

☐ I can choose the correct words to tell what happened **yesterday** and what will happen in the **future**.

☐ I can make a **tally chart** to show how many.

☐ I know that a **square** and a **rectangle** have four sides. A **circle** and **oval** are curved.

☐ I can cut a shape into **halves** and **fourths**.

☐ I know that plants **grow and change**.

☐ I know the names of plant parts: **seed**, **leaf**, **flower**, and **fruit**.

☐ I know that a plant makes food in its **leaf**.

☐ I use **good table manners**.

You did it!

270   271

Answers, pp. 258-271

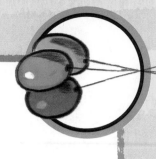

I Did It!

My name is _____.
(Name)

and I am a
Curious Learner!

I finished 12 learning adventures on

_____.
(Date)

Signed by _____
(My mom or dad)

▶ hmhco.com • 800.225.5425

Houghton
Mifflin
Harcourt

A Special Offer for You from
Go Math! Academy

Try it FREE for 2 months!*

*No credit cards required. Registration and acceptance of our Terms of Use and Privacy Policy Required. Limit one free trial per household. Under 18 must get their parents' permission. Continued access after 60 days requires a paid subscription.

Visit gomathacademy.com/workbooks
and enter coupon code GOMATH06

**Catch up,
keep up, or
get ahead!**

Based on the popular curriculum used in classrooms nationwide

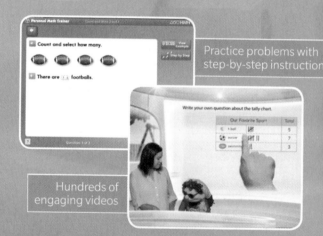

Practice problems with step-by-step instruction

Hundreds of engaging videos

Fun games and rewards to motivate kids

Go Math! Academy™, Houghton Mifflin Harcourt™, and HMH® are trademarks or registered trademarks of Houghton Mifflin Harcourt Publishing Company.
© Houghton Mifflin Harcourt Publishing Company. All rights reserved. 06/14 MS109325